P9-CQI-830

Living Your
Unlived Life

JEREMY P. TARCHER/PENGUIN

a member of Penguin Group (USA) Inc.

New York

Living Your Unlived Life

COPING WITH UNREALIZED DREAMS

AND FULFILLING YOUR PURPOSE

IN THE SECOND HALF OF LIFE

Robert A. Johnson
and Jerry M. Ruhl, Ph.D.

JEREMY P. TARCHER/PENGUIN
Published by the Penguin Group
Penguin Group (USA) Inc., 375 Hudson Street, New York, New York 10014, USA · Penguin
Group (Canada), 90 Eglinton Avenue East, Suite 700, Toronto, Ontario M4P 2Y3, Canada (a division of
Pearson Penguin Canada Inc.) · Penguin Books Ltd, 80 Strand, London WC2R 0RL, England · Penguin
Ireland, 25 St Stephen's Green, Dublin 2, Ireland (a division of Penguin Books Ltd) · Penguin Group
(Australia), 250 Camberwell Road, Camberwell, Victoria 3124, Australia (a division of Pearson
Australia Group Pty Ltd) · Penguin Books India Pvt Ltd, 11 Community Centre, Panchsheel Park,
New Delhi-110 017, India · Penguin Group (NZ), 67 Apollo Drive, Rosedale, North Shore 0745,
Auckland, New Zealand (a division of Pearson New Zealand Ltd) · Penguin Books (South Africa)
(Pty) Ltd, 24 Sturdee Avenue, Rosebank, Johannesburg 2196, South Africa

Penguin Books Ltd, Registered Offices: 80 Strand, London WC2R 0RL, England

Grateful acknowledgment is made for permission to quote the following:

Excerpt from "Little Gidding" in *Four Quartets*, copyright 1942 by T. S. Eliot and renewed 1970 by Esme
Valerie Eliot, reprinted by permission of Harcourt, Inc.
"Last night, as I was sleeping" by Antonio Machado from *Times Alone*, tr. (Wesleyan University Press,
1983). © Antonio Machado. © 1983. Translation by Robert Bly. Reprinted by permission of Wesleyan
University Press.
Excerpt from "Burnt Norton" in *Four Quartets*, copyright 1940 by T. S. Eliot and renewed 1968 by Esme
Valerie Eliot, reprinted by permission of Harcourt, Inc.
"Silently, a flower blooms" by Zenkei Shibayama from *A Flower Does Not Talk*, copyright 1970. Reprinted
with permission by Charles E. Tuttle Co., Inc.

Most Tarcher/Penguin books are available at special quantity discounts for bulk purchase for sales
promotions, premiums, fund-raising, and educational needs. Special books or book excerpts also can be
created to fit specific needs. For details, write Penguin Group (USA) Inc. Special Markets, 375 Hudson Street,
New York, NY 10014.

Library of Congress Cataloging-in-Publication Data

Johnson, Robert A., date.
Living your unlived life : coping with unrealized dreams and fulfilling your purpose
in the second half of life / Robert A. Johnson and Jerry M. Ruhl.
p.   cm.
Includes bibliographical references and index.
ISBN 978-1-58542-586-0
1. Self-actualization (Psychology) in middle age.   2. Middle age—Psychology.   3. Life.
I. Ruhl, Jerry M.   II. Title.
BF724.65.S44J64   2007   2007022969
155.6'6—dc22

Printed in the United States of America
1 3 5 7 9 10 8 6 4 2

BOOK DESIGN BY NICOLE LAROCHE

We shall not cease from exploration
And the end of all our exploring
Will be to arrive where we started
And know the place for the first time.

T. S. ELIOT
FOUR QUARTETS[1]

Contents

Preface

Have you ever yearned for a life different from the one you have?

In the first half of life we are busy building careers, finding mates, raising families, fulfilling the cultural tasks demanded of us by society. The cost of modern civilization is that we necessarily become one-sided, increasingly specialized in our education, vocations, and personalities. But when we reach a turning point at midlife, our psyches begin searching for what is authentic, true, and meaningful. It is at this time that our unlived lives rear up inside us, demanding attention. This book was written to assist you in transforming regret, disappointment, and dissatisfaction into greater consciousness. It presents intelligent ways to explore paths not taken without causing damage to you or others. Using tools and techniques explained in the pages that follow you will learn to:

- Surrender old limitations;
- Enliven friendships, family, and career;

- Unlock new life options and hidden talents;
- Seize the "dangerous" opportunities of midlife;
- Master the art of being truly alive in the present moment; and
- Revitalize a connection with symbolic life, the necessary link between ordinary and enlightened consciousness.

The goal of *Living Your Unlived Life* is to help readers become more attuned to the movements and powers of the invisible world, a world that becomes manifest in our daily lives. Humans require some relation toward the uncharted and mysterious aspects of life that surround us on every side, some orientation not just of the conscious intellect but the whole being. The uniquely human role in the divine drama is to consider and engage these invisible energies, to make them conscious, and to incorporate them into our conduct.

This book draws upon voices spanning cultures, continents, and traditions—from ancient Greek myth to Zen sages to Christian mystics to contemporary poets, artists, and scientists. Our greatest teachers, however, have always been our clients—individuals willing to examine their lives and thereby win their souls. Over the years many people have kindly given permission to discuss their dreams and therapeutic processes. It has been a privilege to share in your journeys. To protect confidentiality, all names have been changed and some information has been blended so that particular individuals cannot be recognized.

Readers will note the use of the singular narrator throughout this book, in references such as "my" clients or to personal experiences. Examples are taken from the lives and therapy practices of both authors. To facilitate understanding, our ideas and stories are combined.

We wish to express appreciation to Liz Williams at WMS Media, for her valuable suggestions and for finding this book a good home; Jeremy P. Tarcher, a publishing legend with whom we are pleased to be associated; Mitch Horowitz at Tarcher/Penguin, for his good faith and support; Leda Scheintaub at Tarcher/Penguin for her mindful editorial skill; and, James Hollis, a kind friend and an articulate Jungian scholar, for his inspirational books and for sharing Liz with us. Appreciation also is due to Roland Evans, Nora Brunner, and, most particularly, Jordis Ruhl, who read early versions of the manuscript and made valuable suggestions as well as provided loving encouragement along the way.

Robert A. Johnson and Jerry M. Ruhl, Ph.D.
May 2007

1

Realizing Our Full
Promise and Potential

A friend of mine recently suffered a miserable demise. He used his money to insulate himself as much as possible from life's sufferings, yet in his final days he was anxious, regretful, angry, bewildered, resentful, and terrified. As he lay dying, his last words were, "If only I had . . ." Hearing such lamentations—the regrets, missed opportunities, lost experiences—is enough to convince anyone to make a survey of their unlived life while there is still time.

Living our unlived life is the most important task in our mature years, to be achieved long before a tragedy shakes us to the bone or we reach our deathbed. To live our unlived life is to become fulfilled, to bring purpose and meaning to our existence.

What is unlived life? It includes all those essential aspects of you that have not been adequately integrated into your experience. We can hear the distant drumbeat of unlived life in the mutterings that go on in the back of our heads: "Woulda-coulda-shoulda." Or in second-guessing our life choices. Or those late-night longings. The unexpected grief that arises seemingly out of nowhere. A sense that somehow we have missed the mark or failed to do something we were so sure we were supposed to do. Where did we go wrong, and what is this life that we find ourselves living, so different from what we set out to do?

We all carry with us a vast inventory of abandoned, unrealized, and underdeveloped talents and potentials. Even if you have achieved your major goals and seemingly have few regrets, there still are significant life experiences that have been closed to you. If you are an only child, then you will never know the experience of having a brother or sister. If you are a woman, then you are not a man, and some of the masculine experience is foreign to you. If you are married, you are not single. If you are a black man, you are not a white man. If you are Christian, you are not Muslim. And so it goes. For everything you choose (or that has been chosen for you), something else is "unchosen."

Consider for a moment something in your life that you cannot do and, as a result, you feel diminished in some way. What do you resent about your life? The endless demands of children or your job? The inattention of your spouse? The limitations of an illness? Whatever seems to be missing—that is part of your unlived life. A woman may decide to pursue a career only to wake up one day, years later, and realize that some part of her always longed to stay home with the children and be a housewife. Or she may discover an aspect of herself that would have chosen a religious life, an existence of reclusive meditation. In the same way a man may feel he has the makings of a poet, but he also has a talent for business and he finds himself climbing the corporate ladder, organizing his life around the business world and supporting a family. Still, the poet in him lives on as a potentiality that he hasn't had time to experience externally.

Perhaps you are short and you always wanted to be tall. Perhaps you wanted to be thin, or to have a different body type, or to explore a musical talent, or to be more athletic. What is unlived yet still has some urgency in you? How is it expressed? As discontent, or anger, or persistant sadness and lack of energy? Are you frequently agitated or disappointed by what life brings you? Do you feel cheated by the circumstances you find yourself in?

Here is another example. Suppose you fall in love with someone outside your existing committed relationship. Some part of you yearns for the excitement, the novelty, and the attentions of this fresh possibility. You feel a genuine attraction; whether it is right or moral, it just comes from somewhere. God made you with erotic desires—, this is a holy fact of natural life and a strong natural drive, but we live in a civilized world that says we must not tear apart people's lives just because we have suddenly been hit by Cupid's arrow. What to do? Act out the attraction every time we see a new person who catches our eye? Deny its existence and fall into a depression? Resent our partners and take it out on them? The truth is that life is not long enough to marry all the people we fall in love with. What are we to do with these unlived passionate desires? From what subterranean place do they arise to take possession of us?

The unchosen thing is what causes the trouble. If you don't do something with the unchosen, it will set up a minor infection somewhere in the unconscious and later take its revenge on you. Unlived life does not just "go away" through underuse or by tossing it off and thinking that what we have abandoned is no longer useful or relevant. Instead, unlived life goes underground and becomes troublesome—sometimes very troublesome—as we age. Of course no one can live out all of life's possibilities, but there are key aspects of your being that must be brought into your life or you will never realize your fulfillment.

When we find ourselves in a midlife depression, suddenly hate our spouse, our job, our life—we can be sure that the unlived life is seeking our attention. When we feel restless, bored, or empty despite an outer life filled with riches, the unlived life is asking for us to engage. To not do this work will leave us depleted and despondent, with a nagging sense of ennui or failure. As you may already have discovered, doing or acquiring more does not quell your unease or dissatisfaction. Stuffing down these rogue feelings or dutifully serving your life's routines will not suffice. Neither will "meditating on the light" or attempting to rise above the sufferings of earthly existence. Only awareness of your shadow qualities can help you to find an appropriate place for your unredeemed darkness and thereby create a more satisfying experience. To not do this work is to remain trapped in the tedium, loneliness, agitations, and disappointments of a circumscribed life rather than awakening to your higher calling.

Life's Conflicting Job Description

We humans are given the most conflicting job description imaginable. We must be civilized human beings, and that requires a whole list of dos and don'ts, culturally determined values such as courtesy, politeness, fairness, efficiency, and all the other virtues—these comprise our duty to society. Family, culture, and the pressures of time push us to specialize, to choose this and not that, and eventually we become one-sided beings. Simultaneously, we are called to live everything that we truly are, to be whole (which means to be hale, healthy, and holy)—this is our duty to the higher Self. This collision of values can make life confusing and painful, though few people are fully aware of the contradictions they live out in the course of a week. We avoid waking up to this inherent conflict because it is too frightening.

A modern person learns to discipline himself, to set the alarm clock to awake early, to go to school and focus upon something on the list of human endeavors from A to Z, from being an artist to being a zoologist. And whatever you decide to do with your life kicks energy into what you decided not to do. Heaven help the person who dedicates his or her life to being good, for inevitably there is a rat's nest of the opposite lurking underground in the shadow world. This is the situation that a modern person finds himself in when he wipes the sweat from his brow at the end of the week and asks, "How can I do this for another day? My life is filled with contradictions. How can I stand the tension?"

Achieving Greater Consciousness

While you can't reel in the years already past, you can go to your unlived life and discover what it would be like to follow different routes from the ones you chose. There are intelligent ways to explore the path not taken without causing damage to you or to others. The reward is achievement of purpose and authenticity.

When brought into awareness, unlived life can become the fuel to propel you beyond your current limitations and into deeper and greater awareness. Your ego and the higher Self join together into a new synthesis. The ego is our name for the center of human consciousness, while the higher Self is a supraordinate organizing principle in the psyche, a centering force for the personality as a total phenomenon.[2]

This is the worthy purpose of the second half of life, the real meaning of growing up. By exploring unlived life we learn to rise above fears, regrets, and disappointments, to expand our vision beyond ordinary awareness, and to embrace the full measure of our being, allowing us to "arrive home," as the poet T. S. Eliot wrote, and "know it for the first time." Harmonizing our conscious lives with the unseen powers that direct the universe brings a sense of "rightness," a feeling of being home even in the midst of our journey.

In some instances you will find an appropriate place to express your unlived potentials externally, rearranging priorities and your outer life. Perhaps you will discover your true vocation or new directions in work or relationships. Often by examining unlived life you will discover that you have actually outgrown old patterns and transcended the need for things that once seemed important. You will gain the power to let go of nagging and negative thoughts and habitual behaviors that hold you back. By exploring what is unlived, you will gain new vitality, energy and affirmation of "what is."

That Reminds Me of a Story

Have you heard about the man with the most powerful computer in the world? He wanted to know whether supercomputers would ever surpass the power of human thought, so one day he wrote in programming language, "Will machines ever be able to think like human beings?" The computer hummed, clicked, blinked, and eventually printed out an answer. The man picked up the resulting message and found his printer had neatly typed the following: "That reminds me of a story."

Stories are rich sources of human insight. Great teaching stories, mythic in nature, portray our psychological condition with indelible accuracy, perhaps with greater precision than the scientific method, which isolates phenomena from their natural context and attempts to deduce cause and effect relationships. Mythic stories tell us holistic, timeless truths, as they are a special kind of literature, not written or created by a single individual but produced by the imagination and experience of an entire culture. Elements peculiar to single individuals may be added or dropped over time, while the themes that are most universal are kept alive. Mythic stories, therefore, portray a collective image—they tell us about things that are true for all people. Mythic images and motifs are encountered and reenacted daily in your home, at your workplace, and on the street corner.

This is contrary to our current rationalistic view of a myth as something untrue or imaginary. While the details of such stories may be unverifiable as historical facts, the essential and underlying truth contained in mythic stories always is profoundly and universally relevant to the human condition. The great novelist Thomas Mann wrote about what it means to become conscious and noted that to tell and live our own life story with authenticity fully brings into view our participation in age-old mythic patterns. "The myth is the legitimization of life . . . only through and in it does life find self-awareness, sanction, consecration."[3] Discovering a mythic pattern that feels connected to one's own life deepens one's self-understanding. This connection also helps one to comprehend how moments in life, apparently accidental, fragmentary, or tragic, belong to the greater whole.

To better understand how we can rise above the human experience of being divided—torn between what is lived and unlived in us—I will draw upon the wisdom from a timeless story, the myth of the two Gemini twins, Castor and Pollux. Their tale will guide our exploration in the coming chapters, illuminating our struggles and showing us, perhaps, a way home.

The saga of Castor and Pollux is an ancient story first recorded in the Heroic age of ancient Greece and believed to be at least three thousand years old. We shall see how Castor and Pollux, unified in their childhood, came to be separated, fragmentary, and miserable. One is cast into the underworld while the other abides in the heavenly realm—and each is inconsolable without the other. After much struggle, they are reunited in heavenly embrace. The evolution of the twin stars of the Gemini constellation serves as a prototype and navigation point for all humans who are on the journey into wholeness.

This story's relevance for our own age is not as strange as it may at first appear. Human biology has not changed much in three thousand years, and the unconscious psyche of the human personality is similar. What it means to be human—to live and to die—has remained stable, although the ways in which our basic needs are met have changed. This is why it is instructive to explore the earliest myths to observe the basic patterns of human behavior and personality. Their portrayal is so direct and simple that we can learn a great deal from them. We can also clearly see in relief the variations peculiar to our own time.

In each of us there is a hidden challenge or wish to reconnect with "the other half," our missing twin, tangible or intangible qualities that we intuitively feel have somehow been lost over the course of a lifetime. We may look for our completion and happiness in the form of a romantic partner, a new job, a different home. In the second half of life the hunger for our missing pieces often becomes acute. It dawns on us that time is running out. So we often set about rearranging things on the outside. Such changes distract us for a time, but what is really called for is a change of consciousness.

In a few hours of lucidity we can see or accomplish half a lifetime of unlived life. The story of Castor and Pollux will show us how to achieve the noble goal of being who and what we were always meant to be.

Castor and Pollux

Castor and Pollux were the sons of Leda, queen of Sparta. In the earliest Greek myths they were known as Castor and Polydeuces, but later they were called Castor and Pollux, and I will abide by these names.

Helen, so famous in history as the cause of the Trojan War, the woman with the face that launched a thousand ships, was their sister. When Helen was first carried off from Sparta, the youthful heroes Castor and Pollux hastened to her rescue. Castor was famous for taming and managing horses and Pollux for his skill in boxing. They were united by the warmest affection, and they were indivisible in all their enterprises.

Though inseparable, Castor was born as a mortal, while Pollux was born immortal. Eventually they grew into adulthood and did what any boys in the ancient world yearned to do; they went through the necessary rites of passage and went off to the wars as a fighting unit. Together they invented the first Greek war dance as a ritual to help carry participants into battle.

Their first big test in the wars came when their beautiful sister Helen was abducted by the Athenian hero Theseus and taken to Attica (southern Greece). Theseus had pledged to marry a daughter of Zeus, and his intent was to hold the twelve-year-old Helen until she was old enough to wed. Theseus, who was fifty years of age, shut Helen away under the care of his mother, Aethra. The twin heroes, however, were furious and promptly set off to rescue their sister. They brought Helen safely home to Sparta, and even set up a rival to Theseus on the throne in Athens. Back in Sparta the two were greeted as conquering heroes, and a great cultural festival was celebrated in their honor. Aethra was made to serve as Helen's slave.

Successful in war, this pair was less fortunate in the affairs of love. While attending a wedding feast, Castor and Pollux fell in love with two maidens, Phoebe and Hilaeira, and ran off with them. Unfortunately, these two young women were already betrothed to cousins of our protagonists. The cousins were, of course, outraged and set after the two heroes from Sparta. In a fight, Castor was killed, and since he was the mortal one, he was destined for Hades. Pollux, too, was wounded, but he was assisted when his father, Zeus, extinguished the foe with a lightning bolt. Finding Castor's lifeless body after the battle, Pollux implored Zeus to be allowed to die with his beloved twin, but this was impossible by reason of his immortality.

Pollux bid farewell to Castor in a ceremony filled with tears, and his mourning was deep. Pollux had never been separated from his brother, and he found it hard to be alone. This was a desolate time, painful and alienating. It was the period of great emptiness and yearning.

Eventually Pollux could not stand existence without his missing half. He was so full of sorrow over the loss of Castor that he had thoughts of venturing down into the underworld.

So our two principal characters, both filled with so much potential and energy, were inconsolable in their separation. One was in the upper world and the other in the underworld. Their cries of unhappiness reverberated throughout all creation. Finally, in anguish, Pollux pled with Zeus to strike a compromise: Could he spend part of his time in the underworld with Castor?

Zeus was so moved by their brotherly love and the intensity of their longing that he made a deal with Hades, the god of the underworld, and thus the split pair could be together again, spending half their time in the nether region and the remainder with the gods on Mount Olympus.

In the beginning this appeared to be a reasonable compromise, a workable solution. Castor and Pollux attempted to live with this arrangement, and they seemed to function tolerably well for a time. But eventually they found it too uncomfortable to live in the other's realm. Castor, the mortal youth, was too uneasy in the abode of the immortals on Olympus, while Pollux, the immortal one, could never find peace in Hades. They were forced to go back to Zeus and tell him that this compromise was not a sufficient solution to the duality of their existence.

Zeus was hard pressed to find a better answer, for the laws dividing mortal and immortal were firmly set. But, after a time, Zeus relented. He declared that there was only one solution—a true synthesis—and he gave immortality to the human youth, Castor, sanctifying him with greater consciousness. Then Zeus set them both in the sky as the sign of Gemini, two components of one unity, in eternal embrace as guiding stars.

A Prototype for the Problem of Unlived Life

I hope you can see this story as a prototype, a navigation point or road map to guide your own journey into wholeness, for it is a presentation and possible solution for the ache that every person carries deep within. We moderns also face the contradiction and division experienced by Castor and Pollux.

As children we begin life whole, and with the grace of God, we return to unity in our mature years. In between, however, is a painful time of division, struggle, and alienation. Early adulthood is devoted to developing an occupation or profession, improving ours earning capacity, learning the social graces, and cultivating relationships. It is a time of outward expansion, as maturational forces direct our growth and the unfolding of our capacities for dealing with the social world. In this process we develop an identity, which we call the ego.

We must work very hard, until exhaustion, just to get ego awareness working well in contemporary life. It takes the whole educational system and all of our socialization processes to promote this consciousness, and our entire society is highly invested in this struggle. However, in the process of becoming differentiated adults, we inevitably become split. We all have both a lived and an unlived life. Most psychotherapies are designed to patch up wounded people and then throw them back into the battle of oppositions. They guide people in how to become better adapted socially: more adept at making money, more highly disciplined, more dutiful, more economically productive. Even when such therapy is successful and gets an individual back out into the rat race again, you can watch them wither over time under the weight of it all.

In the second half of life we are called to live everything that we truly are, to achieve greater wholeness. We initially respond to the call for change by rearranging outer circumstances, though our splitness is actually an inner problem. The transition from morning to afternoon that occurs at midlife calls for a revaluation of earlier values. During the first half of life we are so busy building up the structure of the personality that we forget that its footings are in shifting sand.

Everything human is relative because everything rests on an inner polarity, a phenomenon of energy. There must always be high and low, hot and cold, so the equilibrating process, which is energy, can take place. Everything that conscious human beings experience is brought to us in pairs of opposites. Anything you do or can experience in your life always has some unlived opposite in the unconscious. This is difficult for us to bear. It is not fair. And yet it is true.

It usually takes an abrupt turnaround in attitude for us to profoundly balance our lives. What is required is a synthesis of the conscious personality with essential energies from our unlived life. This is the impetus behind the midlife opportunity. We have differentiated and specialized in egoic consciousness to the point where we can't stand it anymore. In the second half of life we are called upon to examine the "truths" by which we live and even to acknowledge that their opposite also contains truth. It is a mistake to fear that the truths and values of our early adulthood are no longer relevant. They're still relevant, but they have become relative—they are no longer universally true. But to let go of the splitness inherent in modern life would appear to send us crashing into a whirlpool of chaos and relativity, the end of everything that we have most valued.

In order to be complete human beings, we need to recognize that we have an ego, which directs our earthly responsibilities, but also within us is the spark of something godlike. These two qualities seem to yearn to find each other; they want to be united again, as they were in childhood.

Our Connection to the Gemini Twins

Today an increasing number of people feel as if they had another half of themselves, maybe even as in the myth, one part earthbound and practical, the other one living more in another realm, an almost divine plane of existence. Maybe it has to do with what we call the material world and humankind's deep longing for a noble and idealistic side, a spiritual home. The concept of a soul mate existing somewhere is evidence of our search for the missing other.

The mythic story of Castor and Pollux promises a solution, but too many contemporary people have only the first half of the story and ultimately die lonely and meaningless deaths in search of something essential that is unlived but that they intuitively know exists somewhere.

Taking an Inventory of Unlived Life: An Exercise

Take a few moments to consider the following questions:

- How would you title your life story?
- What have been the critical crossroads or turning points in your life?

- When and where have you experienced major losses and disappointments?
- What were some of the missed opportunities or paths not taken?
- What has been the nature of your friendships? Are you a good friend?
- Do you keep a balance of looking after yourself and others?
- Which talents and abilities have you not applied?

In the Appendix at the end of this book you will find an Unlived Life Inventory[4] that is designed to help identify where you are in your life at this moment and what potentials are relatively unlived in you. It does not compare you with other people or offer a prescription for how you should be. The answers to the statements give a snapshot of your experience across four different dimensions: outer, inner, deeper, and greater. Take a few moments to fill out this inventory, score the results, and then reflect upon your life experience.

The benefit of doing this exercise is that it helps you to begin to become conscious of what is unlived yet urgent in you. Then you can begin to do something about it.

2

Divided We Become As Up We Grow

We all are born into a certain situation, given a name, and begin to develop a life. In our early years we take direction from the collective forces around us. There is a lack of freedom in this arrangement, as so many decisions are made for us, dictated by family, society, and tradition. Our relationship with parents is primordial; it sets the tone for all subsequent relationships, but of course the culture we enter also shapes who we become and what is relegated to the underworld of unlived life.

Qualities supported or suppressed are different for each person. A cute little girl enjoys special attention and opportunities at school, while other capacities in her remain dormant. A strong and physically coordinated boy who becomes an athlete may gain social privileges, while other talents go underground. The naturally plump girl in a skinny class will stand out and perhaps even become the brunt of jokes and comments that reinforce her shyness and resentment. The child born with a physical deformity, the sensitive gay boy, the adolescent scarred by acne, the racial minority in an intolerant neighborhood, the brainy kid who loves to read—all individuals face challenges that will bring certain aspects of their personality to the fore.

How we look, how we respond to others, the "goodness of fit" between our innate qualities and that of our parents and teachers, our gender, our social class—all these have enormous impact on what gets included in our lived life and what is relegated to unlived life.

Every culture instills one-sidedness in its members.

The ancient Greeks, whose culture is often referred to as a flowering of Western civilization, called those who did not speak their language barbarians because the sounds they made were unintelligible gibberish—*bar bar*—to their ears. One of the functions of culture is to designate what we pay attention to and what we ignore. We learn to take in some things and dismiss others.

Intelligence, as measured in modern society, is learning to pay attention to the "right" things. And so we make our way through life. A child takes the qualities that the culture likes or calls good and affixes them to the conscious personality, while the remainder falls into unlived life. Often these are quite arbitrary.

Take manners, for example. If I burp loudly at the dinner table, in Western culture this is considered bad manners. Burping, though natural, is socialized out and pushed to the left-hand side of the personality teeter-totter. In many places in Asia if you don't burp at the end of a meal, it is an indication that you are not pleased with the food. Many, many customs are like this. In one place it is a sign of honor to cover your head; in another place it is a sign of honor to uncover your head. In one place it is forbidden to go into a temple or holy place without shoes. If you try to walk into St. Peter's Basilica in Rome without shoes, you will be thrown out, whereas in any village in India you don't dare enter a Hindu temple with your shoes on.

The thrust of Western society is to specialize, with particular emphasis on developing thinking abilities. We ask: What did you get your degree in? To specialize in something means to gather up energy and add it to that faculty of the personality. One robs energy from another faculty to specialize in some aspect that is chosen (or, more likely, one that was chosen for you). In Western culture we are trained in thinking, paid for thinking, honored for our ability to think. In the hierarchy of human skills, thinking currently is at the top of the heap, while feeling and emotional intelligence are considered less important. In other cultures, such as those found in traditional societies such as India, there is a greater emphasis on feeling qualities.

We would like to think there are innate things that are correct, but for the most part it is the result of what significant others have decided for us.

The Influence of the Ancestors

How Castor and Pollux came to be born is key to understanding their destinies. Legend has it that Zeus, king of the gods, was sojourning on the face of the earth looking for a fair maiden, as he liked to do. Being a god and all-powerful, he had his way with a beautiful woman named Leda. *Leda* is not a Greek name, but in Asia Minor it meant "woman." So we could say that out of a union with her divine consort, woman conceived a pair of twins, one feminine and the other masculine. Later that same night Leda also joined in love-making with her earthly husband, Tyndareus, the king of Sparta. From this mortal union Leda simultaneously conceived another pair of twins, one feminine and the other masculine.

In due time, the creations emanating from Leda were brought into this world as quadruplets: One pair, a boy and a girl, had been fathered by a god and mothered by a mortal, while mere mortals parented the other two children. The pair sired by Zeus, the immortal ones, were given the names Pollux and Helen; the mortal twins were called Castor and Clytemnestra. In this manner Leda's children were divided between heaven and earth. A parallel development, though with differences, could be explored through stories of the two women. Our story will focus on the masculine pair, Castor and Pollux.

We can see how the core issues facing Castor and Pollux were created even before their birth. One boy must abide by the practical cultural rules of earth, while the other must be held to the ideals and laws of the heavenly realm. This follows naturally because their mortal mother, Leda, was similarly split; her loyalty was torn between Zeus and Tyndareus. She carried the seeds of twinship and division.

The Swiss psychiatrist Carl Jung wrote that "the greatest burden a child must bear is the unlived life of the parents," by which he meant that where and how our caretakers were stuck in their development becomes an internal paradigm for us also to be stuck. Frequently we find ourselves dealing with a parent's unresolved issues. At times we may replicate the patterns of our ancestors, or we may rebel and attempt to do the opposite. Interestingly, antagonism to the influences of parents binds just as tightly as compliance. Either way, antecedents confine and limit us. Perhaps this fact is behind the ancient biblical admonition that the sins of a man shall be visited "upon the children's children, unto the third and to the fourth generation."

We all are familiar with the phenomenon of the ambitious stage mother who lives out dreams of becoming an actress by pushing her beautiful daughter into beauty pageants by age five, or the Little League dad who plays out his own athletic fantasies to the detriment of his child's development. These are simple examples of unlived life that unconsciously is passed along to the next generation. As long as we unconsciously serve a parent's ambitions, agendas, or limitations, we are prisoners of the past.

Most parents do the best they can, given the tools available to them, but the role of caretaker easily becomes a means and excuse for controlling the life of a child. There always are unconscious assumptions and motivations behind a parent's actions. For example, they may want you to achieve something they missed out on. The unstated bargain is "I will love you if you do what I know is right, but you must not disappoint me."

When a parent cannot stand some quality in his or her child, this is a good indicator of something that is unlived in the parent. I had one client who was not allowed to express anger, though he was regularly beaten for alleged misdeeds. His mother lived her life as a fundamentalist Christian. Anger and sexuality were the work of the devil, so these fell into unlived life. She had to beat these qualities out of her boy to save him. Of course, as an adult this poor man became terribly neurotic concerning these issues; he was promiscuous and carried around a seething cauldron of repressed inner rage, problems that destroyed his first two marriages. The heritage from his family was the suppression of instinctive qualities, and they burst forth at the most inopportune times.

Another example: Nancy came to my consulting room to discuss her marital problems. Her husband and teenage daughter were constantly ignoring and even denigrating her efforts to take care of them. For years she had prided herself on being a good wife and mother, always sacrificing her own needs. How ironic that "these two ingrates," as Nancy called them, were now accusing her of suffocating them. Her demeanor was pinched, anxious, and overtly controlling. This middle-aged woman was constantly nagging her daughter about grades, her friends, practicing the piano. All of this was well intentioned. When we reviewed her own childhood, Nancy recalled how when she was fifteen she watched her mother enter into a midlife fling. Mom abandoned the household, filed for divorce, and then embarrassed everyone by dating a string of younger men. "I swore I would never be like her," my client said, reduced to tearful resentment at the memory. What she came to realize was that she had tipped the teeter-totter of her personality in the opposite direction. Ironically, Nancy was so intent on being the perfect mom that she had given up having a life of her own, which her husband and daughter could plainly see and openly resented. A pattern of rebellion and antagonism to the parental model is just as confining as emulation. The old paradigm distorts and limits present experience in either case.

Suppose you are raised in a family with a fiery and brutal father contrasted by an oversensitive mother who represses all signs of her emotion. A child in such a setting cannot emulate both parents at the same time. When annoyed or stressed, she will be pulled by opposing reactions until a choice is made and one becomes more predominant in her personality. The other personality trait is suppressed, but it still exists as a potential, where it is added to the ever-growing inventory of unlived life. Under stress this person often flips to the opposite, and the suppressed quality comes out in a clumsy, unadapted way.

Inadequate adult modeling narrows our choices, as children naturally imitate what they see. Unfortunately, a child will internalize characteristics of an abusive, frightened, or depressed parent as well as a caring, confident, and happy one. The human brain's capacity for organizing experience through patterned prototypes is both its strength and its downfall. Encountering an early series of consistent experiences can implant a limiting generalization in a child's mind, and so we split off things that we will eventually need to find in ourselves. As children, it is difficult to evaluate whether the larger world runs in accordance with the scheme drawn from the emotional microcosm of the family. This is inevitable in the first half of life. Yet as long as the psyche unconsciously and indiscriminately serves the ambitions, agendas, and confines of others, we fall short of achieving our own potential. Eventually we will be called to sort through this inner maze to find the path that is truly ours. This sorting process, to emerge into an enlarged state of adulthood, is the worthy achievement of the second half of life.

Each individual's temperament and vulnerabilities interact with the mix of ancestral patterns. Another client, Ron, told me his parents had emigrated from the former Soviet Union. "They were Russian, with anarchy inside them. My grandfather was German and his blood flows in me, too. I can feel his correctness in me, the need for order. Sometimes I hold a grudge, but then I say forget it and the Russian blood prevails, the blood of peasants who are used to working. We have to work."

Sometimes unlived life mysteriously seems to skip a generation. I have had several clients who were children of World War II Holocaust survivors. Their parents refused to talk about their experiences in the labor camps, but the children came to me suffering from hopelessness, guilt, and deep depression that seemed unrelated to current life circumstances. "It is as if I must feel the grief that was too much for them to bear," one man told me.

Some people particularly seem to carry compensatory qualities for the partial consciousness of those around them. In the extreme this can be a scapegoat quality: one child becomes the "black sheep" in the family. All families have someplace where unlived life collects.

Something interesting can turn up between siblings in the same family: one child may get an overdose of one quality while a sibling gets an overdose of the opposite. As a result, your brother or sister often carries something that you need in later life. Often we see families in which two siblings can't stand each other, but in adulthood, if they bring enough consciousness to bear, they discover that their personalities need exactly the qualities that their sibling specialized in.

Sigmund Freud said that no one ever really forgives the person who civilizes them; this process leaves indelible influences, scars, and limitations. But if you don't civilize young people and just dump them out naively into the world, this is a worse disaster. So a certain amount of alienation and resentment is inevitable—this is the price of consciousness.

If you are parenting children, making conscious your own unlived life is the best legacy you can pass along to your kids. If you wish to give your offspring the finest possible gift, deal with your own unlived life. One of the most harmful things we can do to others is burden them with our unconscious material, yet we all sin in this manner. The best we can do is to become more conscious of our inner stories, and thereby more understanding of ourselves and of others.

Off to the Wars

As we have seen, Castor and Pollux were inseparable friends throughout childhood, but as consciousness develops there always is division. When we are young and innocent, there is no problem of being divided. Castor and Pollux lived in a Garden of Eden tranquility that had only the beginnings of consciousness and therefore limited psychological difficulties. But as soon as maturity arrives with its complex consciousness, the wars begin.

The Greeks presumed that it was the fate of boys, especially a duo like Castor and Pollux, to go to the wars. They prepared for life's battles by being tested as athletes in the Spartan Games, which was a most sacred event in ancient Sparta, with feats of physical and emotional prowess similar to the Olympic Games. Such games were considered good training for the challenges of maturity.

The wars began in earnest for Castor and Pollux when Theseus from the rival state of Athens carried off their sister Helen prior to her promised marriage to King Menelaus of Sparta. The brothers were called upon to fight, and they successfully brought their sister safely home to Sparta. (Helen would eventually become queen of Sparta, and years later a second abduction of her by Paris would lead to the Trojan War.)

What does this story have to do with modern life? I ask: Is there ever tranquility when there is the stirring of consciousness?

Psychological development automatically creates a conflict within us—these are the inner wars. They vary in character, but the hallmark is always conflict and decision between the righteous and the enemy, the good and the bad, the self and the other, the "this" and the "that" (the word *de-cision* implies a cutting out, just as an incision is a cutting in). These conflicts inevitably create division and anxiety. Our egos can only perceive reality in terms of oppositions, our very language and thought forms being dualistic.

Throughout life all of us are faced with innumerable decisions: some easy and inconsequential, others troublesome and far-reaching. It begins when you wake up in the morning: Should you put on this shirt or another one? Should you go exercise today or conserve energy and focus on your work? Should you eat dessert at lunch or stay on your diet?

It seems that we could not get through life without being divided, and it is this split into lived and unlived possibilities that solidifies our citizenship in the dual world. Everything that conscious human beings experience is brought to us in pairs of opposites.

Another familiar story, the Garden of Eden, speaks of this as the fruit from the tree of the knowledge of good and evil. The underlying conflict that grows out of consciousness is always the same, though with endless variations in the story. The world becomes a warring between this and that, with the ego always caught in the middle and required to choose.

We all go off to the wars each day: at work, juggling the household chores and the demands of the children, the unending oppositions that tie life up in knots. A neurosis consists of entertaining two opposing ideas at the same time, generally one of them conscious and the other unconscious.

The wars will eventually lead to a complete separation of Castor and Pollux, and it is this split that is the seat and dynamics of so many of our problems. Every opposition, every collision, every possibility in your life is basically the dilemma of Castor and Pollux.

What I am calling "the wars" is the duality of ordinary human consciousness. If you watch a child growing, you will see the gradual development of a personality centered by an ego. The ego divides the world into subject and object. "I see this." That subjective "I" grows by watching and imitating others.

Hero Worship and Unlived Potentials

We may see our potentials in an older sibling, a friend, a teacher, a mentor, and that person becomes synonymous with meaning. A person carrying our potential is a hero to us; their smile can raise us to heavenly heights, while a frown hurls us to hellish depths, so great is the power of meaning.

The Castor and Pollux story is filled with hero worship, and it calls to mind our own youthful exploits of growing through imitation of others while taking on the world. The Golden Fleece was the pelt of a golden ram sent to earth by a goddess. It was said to have been placed in a sacred oak tree in the distant land of Colchis. When word went forth throughout the ancient world of Jason's plan to find this priceless treasure, Castor and Pollux were the first to arrive for the adventure, riding all the way from Sparta on beautiful white horses.

A great ship was built to accomplish this sea voyage, and it was named the *Argo*. All the places visited by the Argonauts need not concern us here, but during one stop they were attacked while lighting their fires on the beach of a distant island. A king named Amycus threatened to kill all of the Argonauts unless one would consent to fight with him.

A renowned boxer even as a youth, Pollux had taught the younger Heracles how to fight, but that Greek champion was nowhere to be found during the attack by Amycus and his tribe, the Bebrycians. So the light-skinned Pollux stepped up to do battle with the dark and hugely shaped Amycus. The king of the foreigners, standing on the tips of his toes and rising high above him, tried to bring down his great fist upon the head of Pollux. The young hero swung aside and took the blow on his shoulder. Then he struck his blow. It was a strong one, and under it the king of the Bebrycians staggered and fell down. "You see," said Pollux, "how we keep your law."

The Argonauts shouted with excitement, but it was then that the Bebrycians raised their clubs to rush upon them. The Greeks retreated to get back to the *Argo*, but suddenly Heracles appeared, coming up from the forest and swinging a pine tree with the branches still attached. At this show of strength from Pollux's pupil, the barbarians hurried off, carrying their fallen king with them.

The Argonauts gathered around Pollux and Heracles, saluting them as their champions and placing laurel crowns of victory upon their heads. Pollux had the good sense to thank the gods for the victory (modeling for Heracles the virtue of humility in conjunction with the release of energy that occurs when we exercise new capacities).

In childhood we all have heroes whom we worship because they carry some of our unlived capacities. These may be athletes or celebrities, but often they take the form of someone immediately in our lives. For a ten-year-old boy or girl, the twelve-year-old who lives down the street is often looked up to as a hero. The ten-year-old wants to imitate the older child. He walks like him, or she wears clothes just like her older model. We all know the power of fashion, and especially how fashion runs through a neighborhood of adolescent kids. The style of shoes, the type of haircut, all those things you've got to have. This is a form of hero worship. When we're young we need projections to pull us into life.

Two years later, when the ten-year-old is twelve, he or she has become the characteristics that once were projected onto the twelve-year-old. These potentials have been assimilated and realized. Now he (or she) hero-worships a fourteen-year-old and has a new ladder to climb.

I remember vividly my own early hero-worshipping. It was so strong. Albert Schweitzer was a great hero of mine, chiefly as a musician and a humanitarian. I listened to his recordings. I read his ideas about re-forming recitals of J. S. Bach, suggesting that Bach's works should be performed slowly and deliberately with great ornamentation and attention to detail. I fairly devoured everything about Albert Schweitzer. Then along came this powerful dream in which *I actually ate him.* In my dream I bit into Schweitzer's flesh and then devoured him like a cannibal. This was such a shocking dream that I was embarrassed even to share it. When I told an early mentor about this dream, he patiently explained, "Don't be disturbed. This means you are going to have to be an Albert Schweitzer, in some form. All heroes need externalizing. These are potentials in you that are becoming ripe for development." My life went on to become a pale imitation of Albert Schweitzer's, and that's the power and strength I subsequently gained. At this time I was learning to assimilate my own potential greatness, represented by Dr. Schweitzer.

Eventually I was able to claim my own unrealized potentials rather than always projecting them upon a hero. Schweitzer was a wonderful musician who played Bach in a thrilling manner and published an influential book about building pipe organs. I learned to build clavichords and became an amateur musician, though I played mostly for friends and family. Schweitzer was a medical missionary in Africa, a great humanitarian. Inspired by his example, I have done my best to pursue my own inner work and share my findings with others. For nineteen years I spent my winters in India, attempting to synthesize the best of two very different cultures.

Of course, potentials that are projected and emulated are not all virtues from a societal perspective, and we must not idealize childhood. Children also pick up bullying, coarse language, cruelties, fear, greed, and a host of other "anti-heroic" and limiting qualities by following the lead of older kids, cultural models, and adults. Gang behavior results when youth attempt to initiate each other and assign herolike status to behaviors and values that are inconsiderate or even harmful. Not all of the projected contents of the unconscious are golden.

Romantic Love and Unlived Life

It is important to understand hero worship as the precursor for another archetypal experience by which we all can grow or falter: romantic love. (An archetype is Jung's name for a universal pattern or blueprint by which energies take form. The Greek roots are *arche*, meaning "first" or "original," and *typos*, meaning "model" or "type.") By the teen and early adult years we begin to look for ways to complete ourselves through a romantic partner. Hero worship evolves into a search for our missing pieces by worshipping a soul mate. It is a painful fact that a good deal of what passes for romance is actually our own unlived life reflected back to us.

Take a few moments to look back on your personal relationships. What were the qualities that made your love interests attractive when you first met? What made them shine? The qualities that we most admire in a prospective partner are unlived potentials that are ripe for development within ourselves. When we awaken to a new possibility in our lives, we often see it first in another person. A part of us that has been hidden is about to emerge, but it doesn't go in a straight line from the unconscious to consciousness. It travels by way of an intermediary. We project our developing potentials onto someone, and suddenly we're consumed with him or her. The first inkling that something in us is attempting to change is when we see another person sparkle for us.

Again, this is how we grow, but if we do not become conscious of unlived life, our projections will undermine intimate relationships. As a relationship progresses, so often we demand that others fill in our missing pieces rather than utilize the relationship for mutual growth in consciousness. No one notices at the time, but in-loveness obliterates the humanity of the beloved, for we are really looking at our own incipient potentials. And precisely because we have not reclaimed them as our own, we act out unfinished business and relive old wounds with the very people we profess to love. So often we unfairly require our partners to carry what is unlived in us. By observing what we attribute to the other person, we can see our own depth and meaning.

Love, as practiced from the egocentric perspective, is finding someone to use. "I love you because you are good for me, you complete me." I once heard a client say that she had broken up with her husband because "he doesn't fulfill my needs anymore." Now she wanted to use someone new to get her requirements met. In contrast to this, love is the understanding of the identity of oneself and the beloved. That's the only true union that a human being is capable of realizing; otherwise it is just casting about for mutually agreeable bargains. People think that hate is the opposite of love. Actually, power is the opposite of love. Love is identity with the other, while power is the desire to control the other for our own purposes.

In our culture, mutual projection is regarded as the prerequisite for marriage.

We take for granted that we will marry the person we are in love with, but that doesn't work over time. To fall in love is to give our most profound unlived life to someone to incubate for a while, until we are ready to take it back. But for the relationship to succeed, somewhere along the way each of the partners must take back their projection and reclaim their own unlived life.

Unfortunately, that's usually accompanied by disillusionment.

"You're not the prince I thought you were." "You're not a princess when you wake up in the morning."

As one painfully honest young man recently told me, explaining why he was filing for divorce, "I've fallen out of love. She just doesn't satisfy my soul anymore." I couldn't help myself from replying, "Well, what did you expect?"

If we could just understand that expecting someone else to carry our unlived life is acceptable only for a period of time—until we get stronger—and someday it must come to an end. We aren't wise in this respect, and it's one of the most painful issues in our culture. When, six months or one year or thirty years after the marriage began, the relationship "isn't working," we don't recognize that it's high time for us to withdraw our projections and actually relate to the person—our partner, our spouse.

True relationship can only be based on human love, which is different from romantic love, being in love, or in-loveness.

Romanticism is unique to the West, and only since the twelfth century. And romantic love is not in and of itself a basis for marriage. Our human life, our relationships, are fed by the capacity to love human to human. When we're in love, we put our unlived life—our expectations—on the other person, and it obliterates him or her. There is no true relatedness.

Loving is a human faculty. We truly love someone for who that person is. We appreciate and feel a kinship and closeness. Romantic affection, on the other hand, is a kind of divine intoxication. We deify the other person. We ask that person, without knowing it, to be the incarnation of God for us. Our religious life can be fed by in-loveness. It is a deep spiritual experience, for many people the only religious experience they'll have in life, the last recourse God has to catch them.

When you ask someone in a relationship to incubate your unlived life for you, try to be conscious of what you're doing. If you ask someone to carry that numinous, glow-in-the-dark quality, understand that doing so will obscure him or her from you as a person. Naming the process helps. That's the beginning. Why do I have this feeling when I look at such-and-such a person? Do I really see him or her? Do I truly love this person, or am I putting a bell jar over my beloved, which will obliterate the real person from my sight?

Most of the time we are not conscious of this; our unlived life is bouncing around out of sight and out of control. The extent to which we project in our relationships is a serious problem. We see our own unlived potentials reflected as in a mirror, not the true reality of the other person or the outside world. The exchange of projections takes place much more frequently than you might realize, so you must try to be conscious of it and do what you can to reclaim it as your own. The first half of life feeds on projections— this is how the unconscious becomes conscious. This is akin to the search for the Golden Fleece. If we did not project idealism and love, we might never leave home. However, in the second half of the journey our projected values, hopes, and dreams lose some of their magical power. Our illusions are disillusioned. It must be so if we are to collect our own missing pieces and become more whole.

Reclaiming Ourselves: An Exercise

In this chapter we have seen that how we were raised and who we fall in love with can provide insight into what is unlived in us. The exercises that follow are designed to help you discover clues to the development of your "other side," your "missing twin," as it were, and to assist you in the process of exploring the unlived life of your ancestors. Devote some undisturbed time to these exercises. Make sure it is a quiet world of its own, a sanctuary from outer disturbances.

Let's start with your family of origin. Take a few moments to consider the following questions: What is known about your entry into the world? Was it planned and welcomed or an accident? What stresses might have existed that influenced how you were nourished in those first months and early years? What were the hopes and plans of your parents at this time? Did they have dreams that were deferred?

In dealing with the unlived life of parents, it does no good to resent them. Opposition to parents only strengthens ties to the old family patterns. Try to accept their failings with compassion, without reacting against them. They simply lacked the necessary consciousness to do better with the reality that they faced. Reflecting upon your early upbringing is not about assigning blame but rather a first step in becoming aware of the patterns that continue to shape present experience. Those psychic reflexes might well have been different—and they can still be changed.

Many times people are deeply hurt because they cannot get parental approval. We all have a deep hunger to be understood and accepted for who we are. But when your caregivers cannot provide this, you must accept that this will not be forthcoming. Candidly ask yourself: What difference does their approval or disapproval really make? We all would like it, but, in truth, we don't really need it.

Take some time to answer the following questions, either on your computer or a piece of paper:

- How would you describe your caretakers as they were when you were a child (not as they are now or how you relate to them as an adult)? Use descriptors such as "distant," "preoccupied," "kind," "angry," "loving," "violent," "alcoholic."

- What were the positive characteristics of your mother (stepmother, grandmother, other female primary caregiver) when you were a child?
  - What were the negative characteristics of your mother (stepmother, grandmother, other female primary caregiver) when you were a child?

- What were the positive characteristics of your father (stepfather, grandfather, other male primary caregiver) when you were a child?
  - What were the negative characteristics of your father (stepfather, grandfather, other male primary caregiver) when you were a child?

- What was unlived in the lives of your parents/grandparents? How have their unlived lives burdened your own life? How are you caught in the unlived life of a parent by doing the opposite of what he or she did?

- How have your solutions to these difficulties, developed at an early age, become limited in their effectiveness for your life today?

Now let's look at whom you really admire or the people who were heroic to you in your childhood. Who has mentored you? What qualities did you admire in them? What has been the nature and realization of those qualities in you? Can you see a bit of yourself in the people you put on pedestals?

Finally, a review of your romantic life can yield tremendous information about unlived aspects of yourself. Think back to your first love. What were the things that first drew you to him or her? What about people you had crushes on?

Now turn to your recent or current relationship. What unlived parts of yourself do you unconsciously expect that person to carry for you? Try this: For one day, make a note of your disappointments and frustrations with your significant other. Then see if you can identify those same qualities in yourself. A revealing exercise, to be sure!

After you have finished these exercises, they will keep working silently for you, and you can add to your list. If you want the impact to be greater, return to the exercises over the course of the next several days. Stop to consider the unlived life of your parents right in the midst of everyday activities. Remember how much you idolized your first boss or a special professor in school. Let life be your ever-present test laboratory for discovering how assumptions about reality limit your experience.

3

Midlife: The Call
to Greater Wholeness

We have seen how Castor and Pollux, the Gemini twins, came to be both dead and alive. When Castor was killed in the battle over the stolen brides, the two brothers sought to share the immortal life of Pollux between them.

At the time of Castor's death, Pollux was inconsolable. He prayed that he might also die, and Zeus in pity allowed Pollux to divide his immortality with his brother.

A compromise was worked out, allowing the two to spend half of their time together in Hades and the remainder at Olympus (in Greek mythology, Mount Olympus is considered the home of the twelve Olympians, the principal gods in the Greek Pantheon).

It was this strange request to divide existence between two realms that led Zeus's son Apollo to comment to another Olympian, Hermes:

"I say, why do we never see Castor and Pollux at the same time?"

"Well," Hermes replied, "they are so fond of each other that fate decreed one of them must die and only one be immortal, so they decided to share the immortality between them."

"Not very wise, Hermes. What proper employment can they engage in, that way?"[5]

Indeed. A possible solution to the intolerable split of Castor and Pollux appears to us (as it did for Zeus): Set some time aside for each of these characteristics and see if both can be salvaged in this manner. Such an arrangement initially works tolerably well, with the workdays devoted to one's earthly side and the weekends devoted to fun and play, as well as idealistic and heavenly vision. But soon the symptom of "Thank God, it's Friday" and "Oh, God, it's blue Monday" sets in. Then worse happens if we are conscious enough: The workweek is spoiled by fantasies of the free, heavenly times, and the weekends are more and more burdened with guilt and boredom. Soon the contradictions of our dual character are tying us in knots—and we find ourselves smack in the middle of the "midlife crisis"—or, as I would say, the midlife opportunity.

The Midlife Opportunity

By midlife each of us yearns from a split perspective. And we have an appointment with our missing twin, a personification of unlived life, somewhere down the line. An alert person brings his or her best intelligence to the dryness that sets in as we approach our middle years. If perceptive, we eventually notice that there is more than one side to any human personality: for example, an earthy, instinctive, and practical side and a noble, idealistic side. We sense that somehow we have become separated from something that is essential. One dimension of the personality may cling to safety, predictability, an earthly embrace, while another hungers for ecstatic experience, transcendence, spiritual homecoming.

Between the ages of thirty-five and fifty an important change is underway in the human psyche. Traits that had disappeared since childhood begin to surface. Cherished convictions, morals, and life principles suddenly come under question (if we can stand it). So much unlived life has built up as we approach the threshold of aging that we are overtaken by unsatisfied demands and backward glances.

Concerning this transition, Jung wrote:

The nearer we approach to the middle of life, and the better we have succeeded in entrenching ourselves in our personal attitudes and social positions, the more it appears as if we had discovered the right course and the right ideals and principles of behavior. For this reason, we suppose them to be eternally valid and make a virtue of unchangeably clinging to them. We overlook the essential fact that the social goal is attained only at the cost of a diminution of personality. Many—far too many—aspects of life which should also have been experienced lie in the lumber-room among dusty memories." [6]

With aging we all face threats to our capacity to control outcomes. Perhaps it is the painful onset of physical limitations (our bodies no longer respond instantly to our every command), the death of parents and even friends, or disillusionment of youthful dreams—all these may contribute to a mental shift at midlife from "time since birth" to "time left until death," and we begin to feel that time is running out while something essential is still missing.

It is a truth that anything undertaken on the face of the earth entangles us in the field of time. For example, when you marry you have set aside entire blocks of your life. For most of us this includes getting up in the morning to keep a paycheck coming, four a.m. feedings of infants, time spent transporting the children to and from school, doctor appointments, sports practice, play dates. When midlife comes, most contemporary people begin to have thoughts of extricating themselves from this jail of time (that they have worked so hard to build), and the primary issues revolve around not having enough free moments.

Nature's Way of Turning Us Around

Jung borrowed an ancient Greek word, *enantiodromia*, to describe the turning to the opposite at midlife. The word means "counter" (*enantio*) "running" (*dromia*). The philosopher Heraclitus used this term to describe the play of opposites,[7] and taught that in time everything turns into its contrary: Out of life comes death and out of death life, out of the young comes the old and from the old come the young, out of waking comes sleep and out of sleep waking. This is the stream of creation and dissolution. Enantiodromia occurs when an extreme, one-sided tendency dominates conscious life; in time an equally powerful counterposition is built up in unlived life. At first it interferes with conscious performance, but in time it breaks through conscious control. Chinese philosophy formulated this process as the interplay of yin and yang.

It is as if key aspects of our personality teeter-totter become so one-sided by midlife (unlived life reaches a critical tipping point) that the personality attempts a correction to restore balance.

We could compare the human life span to the course of the sun. In the morning our lives gain in strength until they reach the zenith in the heat of high noon. Then comes the turning to the opposites. "The afternoon of life is just as full of meaning as the morning; only, its meaning and purpose are different," Jung commented.[8]

Researchers argue over whether the midlife crisis is a universal phenomenon of modern life, but we do know that so often by middle age the cultural process has become very dry for us, as if we have wrung all the energy out of our character. This is true not only when life has disappointed you and achievements have fallen short of expectations, but also if you have accomplished a good measure of success. Meanwhile, the energy of your unlived life becomes more urgent.

In our middle years we become vulnerable to new doubts, anxieties, and moods. We may suddenly fall in love, break up a marriage, storm out of a job in desperation. We may begin to feel empty, trapped in a life that seems to be living us. These are "dangerous" moments, but they can set the stage for a whole new phase of development. It begins to dawn on us, if we pay attention, that something more is needed.

The arrangement by which couples unconsciously agree to cover for each other's unlived lives is often blown apart in the middle years, complete with recriminations, misunderstandings, and the release of long-repressed resentments and pent-up emotions. It is so easy to look for someone else to blame, even when we have participated in our one-sided development. Divorce, affairs with younger and seemingly more attractive partners, sudden career changes—all are common during this time. Yet we fail to recognize them as symptoms of our souls seeking balance.

On the surface at least, to stay unconscious seems like a safer choice, to redouble our efforts to achieve happiness based on the formula prescribed for the first half of life: Strive after possessions, career achievements, ego enhancements. We may think that choosing something new or better will quell our discontent and desire. Yet to remain prisoner to a provisional fragment of the personality results in serious damage, and you are going to suffer either way. Beneath our cultural fantasy of health—too often equated with becoming socialized to some imagined normal or average state sanctioned by society—is a commitment to stability at the expense of authenticity.

The philosopher Friedrich Nietzsche explored the burden of the unlived that is not reclaimed:

Zarathustra goes to the grave with the unfulfilled dreams of his youth. He speaks to them as if they were ghosts who have betrayed him bitterly. They struck up a dance and then spoiled the music. Did the past make his path so weighty? Did his unlived life impede him and consign him to a life that seems not to pass?

Coming to Terms with Failure

At midlife we come face to face with our failures and losses. As we age, each of us is confronted by limitations, threats to our capacity to control outcomes, and deflations of our presumptions of omnipotence. We may remain on the surface of life or we may learn that existence is much deeper, less controllable, more mysterious and miraculous than previously understood.

The Spanish poet Antonio Machado writes of turning the failures of the first half of life into meaning in our later decades:

Last night as I was sleeping,
I dreamt—marvelous error! —
That a spring was breaking out in my heart.

I said: Along which secret aqueduct,

Oh water, are you coming to me,

Water of a new life

That I have never drunk?

Last night, as I was sleeping,

I dreamt—marvelous error!—

that I had a beehive

here inside my heart.

And the golden bees

were making white combs

and sweet honey

from my old failures.

Last night, as I was sleeping,

I dreamt—marvelous error!—

that a fiery sun was giving

light inside my heart.

It was fiery because I felt

warmth as from a hearth,

and sun because it gave light

and brought tears to my eyes.

Last night, as I slept,

I dreamt—marvelous error!—

that it was God I had

here inside my heart.[9]

(Translation by Robert Bly)

Exploring Paths Not Taken

Most of us can recall a class reunion—that institutionalized venue for parading one's accomplishments and reflecting upon one's life. We encounter former schoolmates who were promising youngsters but who, years later, seem to have grown cramped in the carapace of an adolescent persona. This is the result of clinging to the identity won in early adulthood.

One of my clients, Jeanine, recently attended her thirtieth high school reunion. "It was really depressing," she told me. "There were so many people who were desperately looking to change their lives. One guy, who was a star athlete in high school, had bought into the family printing business and now at the age of forty-eight realized he hated printing. He was in the middle of a divorce and had decided to join the forest service. Another gal, who was the life of the party in our youth, now seemed like a drunken floozy; she wore a low-cut sweater, drank too much, and threw up in the bathroom at the reunion dinner. I overheard her tearfully telling a classmate, 'You didn't make all the mistakes I did.' Her friend responded, 'Oh, I made them all right, I just didn't marry them!' "

Jeanine concluded that she had been pretty lucky, successfully switching careers in her thirties and then starting a successful marriage. "Thank God I stopped drinking and started to grow up at thirty-five," she said. "Many of my classmates are still stuck in that high school mentality." But still, Jeanine felt vaguely dissatisfied with her life. "I have an abundance of riches, but still I can identify with the lyrics of that old song: 'Is that all there is?'"

Another client, Jack, was a multimillionaire, retired from a company he built, when we met. As part of a golden parachute agreement, he continued to receive a handsome annual salary for consulting with his company's board of directors, but he soon found that the new chief executive didn't really want his advice. Jack had effectively been put out to pasture. He was bored, lonely, and lacking in purpose—like many people disappointed and disillusioned by some realities that may come with retirement. He spent several sessions with me bragging about his financial success, friends in high places, vacation homes, and priceless antique collections. He seemed to need an audience. When I could get a word in, I tried to suggest that the qualities that had taken him so far were inadequate for the next stage of his life. "Yes, yes, you're right," he would say, and then promptly forget my suggestions. Half-jokingly he would tell me of grandiose daydreams he had for rebuilding areas in Southeast Asia decimated by the giant tsunami that struck there. Unfortunately, he would not take the smallest step toward realizing such projects or even contemplate what was undeveloped and unlived inside him. He was heavily invested in his role as the "big man," and lived in stories of the past.

I have also met many female equivalents of Jack, women striving to hold on to their physical beauty, which they have used as a bargaining chip to lure men like Jack. There is an inherent sadness, bitterness, and inappropriateness that accompanies clinging to the persona of youth. (As will be discussed at length in chapter 8, a youthful spirit and sense of new possibilities is essential at any age, but avoidance of the call to evolve into a broadened consciousness keeps us from realizing authenticity.) Our desire to be taken care of and protected is understandable, but bowing to dependence is a refusal to grow up, an abrogation of our full potential.

Most of us work so hard to obtain an identity that it becomes very hard to let it go. When we see how stubbornly youthful illusions and assumptions and egoistic habits persist years later, we gain an idea of the energies that were needed to form them. The guiding ideas and attitudes that led us into life, for which we struggled and suffered, become part of who we are, and so we seek to perpetuate them indefinitely.

But what worked in the first half of life is nearly always inadequate for the challenges of our mature years. How we make sense of a situation at age five or even twenty-five is pretty limiting, even primitive, when we reach the age of forty-five or seventy-five. Why should we believe that the attitudes and responses that sufficed during one stage of life would be adequate for the challenges of subsequent stages?

The ancients had a word for this; they called it *hubris*, which is sometimes translated as "pride" or "arrogance." It implies a limited knowledge, a partial perspective coupled with the presumption that one knows the whole story. It is a self-deception, as analyst James Hollis has pointed out.[10] When you think you know the whole of what is going on, you most likely are acting out of a complex (a one-sided inner pattern). The story we consciously know, or believe we know, is never the whole saga that is unfolding within and around us. In the first half of life most people suffer from hubris. Given time, life has ways of correcting this human fault through suffering, as we are shown in the classic Greek tragedies.

Descent into the Domain of Hades

In our guiding myth, Pollux, in a desperate ploy to stay connected with his brother, follows Castor into the underworld, where a deal is made with Hades.

Hades is an ancient god whose name means "unseen." Since he is ruler of the underworld, his domain also came to be known as Hades. Located just below the surface of the earth, Hades is where the souls of the dead reside, remembering their earthly lives. These souls were known to the Greeks as shades. We moderns don't have a very good concept of Hades; we clumsily call it Hell, but for the ancients it wasn't so much a place of punishment as a place of colorlessness.

Hades keeps order in the underworld; he was given that area to oversee at the time when Zeus was given the Olympian realm and Poseidon took hegemony over the sea (observe that Zeus and Hades are brothers). The god Hades is seldom represented on surviving Greek relief sculptures and vases from ancient times, and this is no accident. Hades' original name, Aidoneus, translates as "the unseen one." As lord of the underworld, he inherently inspires both fear and fascination. People were cautious about even uttering his name, so the ancients invoked his presence with euphemistic titles such as Trophonios (the nourisher), Polydegmon (the receiver of many guests), Euboulos (the good counselor), and Plouton (the giver of wealth—hence the Roman name *Pluto*). The dramatist Sophocles referred to Hades as "the rich one."

These names suggest that Hades and the underworld are symbols not merely of loss and demise but also of wealth. The lord of the underworld is a creatively transformative figure, the male counterpart to Demeter, the fertility goddess who brings forth the grains and fruits of the earth. Indeed, immersion in this realm yields an inner fruitfulness. Psychologically speaking, we must go to the underworld to recover riches.

Many of the Greek heroes made the treacherous journey into the depths, either to question the shades or to free them. In our guiding myth of Castor and Pollux, it is important that for a critical period the duo spend half their time in the underworld. In a similar manner, it is only through exploring what is unlived that we can resolve the dualities that become so troublesome as we age. When we have attained sufficient life experience—and often concurrently are driven by disappointments, dissatisfactions, and desperation to consider alternatives—then the descent to Hades is undertaken. Avoidance of an examined life keeps us in a form of spiritual adolescence, protected from a real engagement with soul.

In modern psychological parlance we refer to shadelike denizens of the underworld as complexes—unconscious figures that are colorless, repetitive, and separated from the dynamic flow of life. That which is unconscious has power over us, influencing our choices and limiting our experience through programmed habits.

For the Greeks of ancient times, Hades was the realm where souls stirred amid the unchanging, redundant, disembodied, "dead" weight of the past. The riddance of ghosts by means of placation was an important element in ancient notions of sacrifice and purification. As we moderns explore the underworld, we, too, encounter stagnant and stale backwaters of the personality—but also soulful possibilities. We, too, must placate troublesome ghosts of the past.

Complexes Go Round and Round

Although our conscious minds think they are running the show, much of the activity involves accepting or vetoing decisions that are already made beneath consciousness. Psychological research suggests that decisions are normally made by unconscious processes a half second before we are conscious of them. Jung identified these invisible inner processes nearly a century ago, and he called them *complexes.* (The developmental psychologist Jean Piaget later called them *schemas*, while neuroscientists currently describe such phenomena as neuronal networks. The metaphor changes, but the archetypal reality of the underworld is ever present).[11]

Complexes articulate our reality, influence our moods, and make us anxious, depressed, regretful, and even ill. Worst of all, they interfere with our natural ability to creatively respond to change. They hold us to repetitious patterns of response. The word *complex* has passed into common speech. Nowadays everyone knows that people "have complexes." Jung defined a complex as a group of psychic patterns, potentially both positive and negative, infused with strong emotion. Where did these repetitive core ideas of thought and emotion come from? Past experience. We have complexes because we have a history. We continue to interpret present reality on the basis of established patterns—and some of these are nonadaptive and suboptimal. Yet they become built-in structures, ways for interacting and making sense of the world. We continue to make boring, self-defeating, or limiting choices in life, to curse bad luck or fate, all the while failing to recognize that we are serving old unconscious programs.

It is not pathological to have complexes. However, a one-sided complex is the hammer in your tool kit that you use over and over whenever something needs fixing when perhaps a screwdriver would work better.

At midlife, hopefully, you have gained enough life experience to reflect upon your history and enough psychic strength for the ego to begin critiquing itself. With some help you can discern hidden motives and old agendas and identify those aspects of unlived life that need repair work. You won't need to search very far. Complexes make themselves known through disturbing dreams, emotional outbursts, moods, and all kinds of self-limiting behaviors.

Do you keep bumping into the same reality? Can you see similar cycles or patterns in your relationships or on the job, even after switching partners and employers? Is it possible you have become so set in your usual ways of seeing life that you rely on habits that limit what is possible? As the novelist Flann O'Brien observed, "Hell goes round and round. In shape it is circular and by nature it is interminable, repetitive and very nearly unbearable." This is how a complex can feel when we are under its influence.

How We Remain Stuck in Old Habits

Nearly a century after Jung introduced his theory of complexes, neurologists and researchers are now gaining a clearer understanding of how these inner patterns operate. The human brain is made up of an estimated one hundred billion tiny nerve cells called neurons; they provide cell-to-cell signaling and reach out to other neurons to form networks. The pattern of signaling in a system of neurons is the foundation of thought. To make a memory, a neuronal network links together concurrently firing neurons into patterns. Pathways that occur frequently create the building blocks of the personality.

Neurons that fire together develop a bond with one another and therefore are more likely to fire together again. Based upon these patterns we essentially tell ourselves a story about how the outside world is. Any information we take in from the environment is colored by the experiences that we have already had and the emotional response we were having at the time.[12]

In this manner what we *have seen and felt* dictates what we *can see and feel*.

Julie was forty-three years old when she came to see me. She was a registered nurse and had recently become engaged to Barry, who owned a successful roofing company. "I'm afraid I will mess up the marriage," Julie told me. She revealed how fear of failure and an unforgiving perfectionism had driven and dominated her life for decades. The oldest of eight children, Julie grew up in Southern California. Her mother was a busy and successful minister, and her father had been an "out-of-work intellectual" who was responsible for raising Julie and her seven younger siblings. As the oldest child, Julie took on enormous responsibility at a young age, serving as the de facto mother in the family, particularly after an incident that occurred when she was only eight. During a family beach vacation she found her four-year-old sister facedown in the water. Julie screamed for help, but no one came. As was often the case, her parents were preoccupied with their own activities and had left the two girls to play unattended. Panic-stricken, Julie pulled her little sister to dry land and found an adult down the beach to help resuscitate her. "From that day, I knew that I had to be vigilant," Julie said. "The world was not safe."

The overpowering emotions that Julie felt that day on the beach at the age of eight—fear, shock that the adults in her life couldn't be trusted to keep things safe, a sense of responsibility for her sister—became her primary paradigms for being in the world. They propelled her into a career as a nurse, where she dealt effectively with other people's trauma on a daily basis. She was a perfectionist, a self-described "control freak" who paid attention to every detail. Julie felt okay as long as she was at work, but when she went home her hypervigilance could not be turned off. She had recurrent dreams in which a small girl was running joyfully through a meadow, "but she goes too fast, isn't watching, and falls off a cliff."

Intimate relationships had always been problematic for Julie as an adult. Men complained that she was too intense and controlling. After two decades of short-term romances, she wanted real intimacy with Barry but was terrified of commitment. Could he be trusted? Even on a simple holiday vacation she worried that he would not adequately provide for her—she had to make all the arrangements and it ended in a quarrel. That inner circuit representing the thought "the world is not safe . . . you must be vigilant" continued to operate in Julie's head and to shape her daily experience of life.

By reworking this reflexive pattern, over time Julie became

more trusting of others, and her complex was reformulated with a different resolving outcome. Her wedding took place, and eventually she even retired from nursing and found a new career in which she was not immersed in life and death situations on a daily basis.

Another client, Peter, came to me recently and said he had a "Miss Algren dream." Peter dreamed over and over that his high school math teacher was assigning him a failing grade. Even though he had earned a Ph.D. as an adult and was professionally accomplished, he still suffered the nighttime anxiety of a confrontation with Miss Algren every time he got into a particular type of situation. He was no longer in danger of flunking a class, but the complex organized around fear of failure was an active and ongoing disturbance in my client's life—decades after high school. This habitual pattern was in need of repair, reparation, and rehabilitation. Through inner work Miss Algren's tyranny was eventually disarmed. Then the dreams stopped.

At first, most people will deny how much of their life is controlled by complexes. It is the delusion of our egos that we know all we need to know and we are in control. Jung wrote: "Consciousness behaves like someone who hears a suspicious noise in the attic and thereupon dashes down into the cellar, in order to assure himself that no burglar has broken in and that the noise was mere imagination. In reality he has simply not dared to go up into the attic."

It is not so much that we have complexes; it is more accurate to say that complexes have us—these fixed patterns of response have a degree of autonomy that allows them to break in against the wishes of consciousness.

Yesterday's Solution Is Today's Problem

It is important to remember that complexes begin as adaptive strategies; they are aimed to produce logical outcomes based on the core ideas and premises at the time they were formed. But what worked as yesterday's solution often becomes today's problem simply because it is so one-sided. The patterns you have adopted in the first half of life are reference points, providing a baseline for organizing your experience. Too often they become obstacles to further development.

When we are working with complexes, the goal is not to eliminate patterned thoughts and behavior but rather to loosen them up sufficiently to uncramp the conscious mind and give us more freedom of choice, to regain access to lost resources that are essential to a more fulfilling life.

When you shine the light of consciousness on complexes, they are no longer invisible, and they can begin to evolve. Once you recognize that a certain reflexive response happens, you can slow down, reflect, and catch yourself. This takes practice, and it can be frustrating at first. It requires humility. To disarm a complex you must learn to move your ego into a position of witness, letting go of any illusions of omnipotence you might have. In the next chapter I will describe a method to help accomplish this by quieting the noise in your mind so that you can observe your own mental processes.

The Paradox of Identity

It may come as a surprise to realize that the ego itself is a complex; it is a kind of meta-pattern that directs all the other patterns that have accumulated in our lives. We become so closely identified with this "I" that we come to think it is who we really are.

Our minds utilize fixed reference points to make sense of processes whirling around and flowing through us. Each perception is an edited and abstracted version of what is actually out there. If we think about the shifting scenery too long, we become disoriented. Like a dancer or a child on a merry-go-round, we must fix our eyes on something solid so as not to become dizzy and lose our balance. As a matter of utility, we rely upon patterns to make our experience coherent, but ordinary convictions and common sense assumptions also limit us.

And it is here that we run into a paradox. As we create ourselves, it is inevitable that life will move into particular structures and forms, into defined and defining patterns of organization. Structures and a sense of content are necessary for life to cohere. Pathways and habits develop, and over time they become boundaries, limiting our freedom and narrowing our experience. Our choices become increasingly restricted as we rely upon what is familiar and as we strive to be consistent with who we already are or how others expect us to be. Our thoughts and behaviors reference a self-identity—the ego.

We do our best to catch hold of life by acting as if it is stable and unchanging. We seek structure, form, and meaning, and then we become limited by our structures, forms, and meanings. In truth, the ego with which we identify is an accumulation of old habits conditioned by past experience and held together by the paper clips and chewing gum of memory. It does its best to make our experience safe and predictable, but it also can inhibit us. This is the paradox of identity.

Cultural institutions can also run afoul of the paradox of identity. Businesses, governmental agencies, colleges, and religious institutions all can become resistant to change when they are constrained by identities. You may have experienced this type of scenario in the early formative years of an organization. At first its members are open to "whatever works"; initially there is great freedom and flexibility in responding to an ever-changing environment, but over time success brings rules, regulations, procedures, and roles. Eventually spontaneity, risk, and excitement are gone. The provisional identity becomes institutionalized. Instead of a makeshift experiment into what is possible, we start to act as though it (the identity) is really real.[13] This is the predicament of all identities—habits that nature has gotten herself into become structural.

There is a joke in which Satan is talking with one of his fallen angels while looking at the foibles of humans on the earth. "What should we do?" implores the helper. "See there, a human has gotten hold of a piece of truth!" Unperturbed, the Prince of Darkness replies, "Don't worry, these humans will try to institutionalize it, and then it will belong to us again."

By midlife your identity is the institutionalization of your past. You have good reason to be attached to it, but it is not all of who you are meant to be. By reflexively living in the past you miss the fullness of the present. The movement of energy into structure (having an ego) is necessary for life to cohere. We need form, yet we are best served when the conscious personality is capable of ongoing course correction through dialogue with the dynamic unconscious.

A Revaluation of Values

We have seen how our choices in the first half of life are made under the influence of genetic and cultural influences, particularly examples set by Mom, Dad, teachers, heroes, and our love interests. We acquire an identity and a repertoire of patterned ways for making sense of and responding to the world.

But one morning we wake up and feel as if something important has been lost along the way. Then we are called upon to examine the truths by which we live and even to acknowledge that their opposites also contain truth. As Jung pointed out, it is a mistake to fear that the truths and values of early adulthood are no longer relevant; they have just become relative—they are not universally true. But to let go of the splitness inherent in the process of becoming conscious would appear to send us crashing into a whirlpool of chaos and relativity, the end of everything that we have most valued.

It is curious how modern people will go to almost any length to stay busy and thereby avoid examining unlived life. Contemporary people have a nearly insatiable appetite for amusements and addictions—to drugs, food, television, shopping, wealth, power, and all the other diversions of our culture. For many years I believed that our avoidance of soulful engagement is the result of a fear of being overtaken by "uncivilized" qualities from the unconscious. But I have come to understand that we resist our highest potentials even more persistently than we reject our so-called primitive energies.

Much of what remains undeveloped in us, psychologically speaking, is excluded because it is too *good* to bear. This may seem silly, but if you look honestly at your life, you will find it to be true. We often refuse to accept our most noble traits and instead find a shadow substitute for them. For example, instead of living with spirit, we settle for spirit in a bottle. In place of our god-given right to the ecstatic, we settle for temporary highs from consuming something or possessing someone. At first it is puzzling why we would look for our potentially best qualities in something or someone else. From the point of view of the ego, the appearance of a sublime trait or quality might upset our whole personality structure.

In going down into the underworld a person of integrity can draw the skeletons out of the closet fairly easily, but he will likely fight to the end of his neurotic strength to hide the divinity of his own being. It is heartening to learn that inner work at midlife is not just unrelieved darkness; it also brings out some of the finest values. Hades is not just the abode of loss, lament, and depression; it is a transformative realm, filled with riches, promising a new harvest of life potential.[14]

Where Are You Stuck? An Exercise

We all have places where we cut ourselves off from potentially exciting and fulfilling experiences due to habit, fear, or laziness. A simple way to locate some of your complexes (which are, by definition, unconscious) is to reflect upon the past week and notice what situations disturbed you. Where did you have a run-in with someone? When and how did you procrastinate or avoid something? Perhaps you failed to speak up for yourself or steamrolled over someone (power complex). Did you constantly sacrifice your own needs while trying to please others? Did you overcompensate by boasting or belittling others (inferiority complex)? Maybe it involved paying bills (a money complex). Did you repeat a pattern of isolating yourself from the potential support of friends and community (outsider complex)? In what ways did you fail to engage life fully? Sometimes this is called the mother complex—wanting to stay infantile and half asleep. The mother complex is observed when a parent holds too much sway in the child's development; it may or may not be tied to a specific gender. What do you rarely talk about with others? Why is this so? Are you embarrassed? Do you want to avoid conflict? When do you feel uncomfortable, nervous, or sensitive?

Unlived life will be projected onto others to the extent that it is unrecognized. What you devalue and reject in yourself you will criticize and castigate others for. What you fear in yourself you will fight or flee in others. What you lack in yourself you will depend upon others to provide.

There are a diverse number of complexes, as many as there are typical situations in life. Recall that these clusters of experiential energy are trying to protect you and simplify your choices by drawing upon past experience, but they also limit your freedom and bind you to the past. They are fallacies of overgeneralization. You cannot be rid of complexes, but you can loosen them up and broaden your repertoire of response.

To change these repetitive core ideas will require more and greater awareness. Purchase a notebook and begin noting when, where, and how you feel stuck, limited, or diminished.[15] In becoming aware of the effects of your complexes, it is not helpful to judge yourself or get frustrated. Simply by bringing more awareness to these underworld processes, your life will begin to change. Whenever you let go of an old, restrictive program, your unlived potential emerges more fully.

4

Learning the Timeless Art of Being

To question the shades of Hades—what we contemporary people call complexes—we must create a still observation deck from which these underground energies can be witnessed; otherwise they reflexively have their way with us. When our lives are filled with frantic *doing*, we are generally driven by patterns from the past. Only by learning and practicing the timeless art of *being* can we dis-identify from and begin to change one-sided complexes and realize deeper and greater awareness.

One reading of the Castor and Pollux story is to understand the brothers as symbols of our terrestrial and divine natures. The earthly realm of Castor is defined by doing. We have all kinds of daily activities—from paying our bills to calling up a friend on Saturday night to go out on the town. Certain life tasks are best served by doing. Washing the dishes, vacuuming the carpet, balancing the checkbook—clearly these are doing activities. But there are other aspects of life that require equal time in the realm of being, and this includes relationships, love, and sensing the sacred in our daily experience, noticing the miraculous in a slant of sunshine, a bird's song, or an act of human kindness.

Midlife is a time of reappraisal, in part because as we age the realm of being must become more predominant. We have enough practice at doing in the world by this time so that we can put a portion of our daily activities on automatic pilot and invest some energy into learning the power of presence.

In our busy lives we all require time and place to connect to something greater and more enduring than our own egos, an entity or force that is immortal and timeless (Castor yearning for Pollux). We need a practice of some sort because doing and being become so painfully separated in modern life. The antidote is to set aside time for reflection, contemplation, and focused presence. This is not mindlessly daydreaming, zoning out, or going into a stupor. It is from a state of energized being that we realize the highest potentials in any situation.

At times midlife can feel like the experience of adolescence all over again. To be caught between identities is a vulnerable, frightening position. We may question who we are and ask ourselves: What is the purpose of my life? I used to joke with middle-aged friends that I was going to set up a recorded greeting on my answering machine that would announce: "At the tone please tell me who you are and what you want [pause] and if you know how to truly answer such questions, then you are a genius of the second half of life."[16]

Which of these two aspects of the human job description is more important: finding your purpose in the outer, earthly realm (getting to work on time, finishing projects, paying your taxes) or serving your higher purpose in the eternal realm (finding time for beauty, love, spiritual pursuits)? To side with either one at the exclusion of the other results in a painful Castor-Pollux split.

Your life has many outer, earthly purposes: the demands of your job, supporting your family, achieving financial stability. Outer purposes are important and necessary, but they are also impermanent, relative, and constantly shifting.

In the second half of life it is not so much what you do that matters; it is the level of consciousness that you bring to your doing. This is to share time with the gods on Olympus.

You can invite being into your life. You can create space for it to occur. It is important to reestablish your zero point periodically. That is the meaning behind a Benedictine ritual: Benedictine monks stop whatever they are doing seven times a day and go into the chapel to get quiet and reestablish zero. Then they go back out and invest themselves in the world again. Their outer purposes can then be aligned with their greater inner calling. Bringing the calmness and focus of being into doing activities is a supreme achievement. If your mind has big ideas of progress, they will just get in the way. It will be like learning a foreign language; you cannot grasp it all at once, but by repeating the exercises described in this chapter you will gradually master it, and you will attain a wonderful new power.

When you are confused or are feeling sad, lonely, or restless, the best prescription is not to get lost in more activity but simply to sit down and be still. Notice your breathing. Is it shallow and in the top of your chest, or is it full and relaxed?

As you get physically still, you will notice the monkey chatter that goes on continually in your head. You can't get to zero by shrieking "QUIET!" at yourself. Buddhists say that the wheel of illusion is spinning away and anything you do to try to stop it just turns it faster. So stop and watch the spinning of your mind until it uses up its energy and slows of its own accord.

Resisting Cultural Pressure to Do More, Go Faster

There is a deep fear in our culture that if we stop or even slow down, someone else will catch us or even pass us in the rat race of life. The term 24/7 is used today as shorthand in advertising and increasingly in conversations to indicate around-the-clock commitment. "This deodorant will protect you 24/7," or "I'm on the job 24/7/365." This is the collective thought. It does not allow for stopping, for standing still.

I like to swim at the local YMCA; I am a regular there and many people know me. Not long ago one of the lifeguards saw me coming; and her manager had told her that I write books, so she approached me to ask for an inspirational quote to copy on the blackboard for the people who were exercising. I thought for a moment, and a proverb from the *Upanishads* came to mind: "By standing still we overtake those who are running." The teenager heard me out, thought for a moment, and then replied, "No way!" She walked to the blackboard and instead wrote: "Go, go, go!"

We live in a "go, go, go" society. It is increasingly difficult to find a moment of repose. At the airport television monitors flash the news at you from every corner. In stores and restaurants music and flashing visual displays bombard the senses. I recently had the opportunity to experience being in an isolation tank (also commonly known as a sensory deprivation tank), which is a lightless, soundproof tank in which subjects float in salty water (denser than the human body) heated to skin temperature. These tanks are used to test the effects of sensory deprivation and also for meditation, prayer, and relaxation, and in alternative medicine.

This seemed like an excellent place to get away from the busyness of modern life, and a friend convinced me that it would be a soothing and peaceful experience. When the metal door was closed, the tank felt a bit like a coffin, but I appreciate solitude and was looking forward to the quiet. Within seconds, however, sentimental and redundant music of the worst sort was pumped in through a small speaker in the chamber. I had to endure that music for nearly twenty minutes. When at last they opened the door, it took all the self-control I could muster not to tear into the operator. I asked why in the name of God they played music, and I was told that most people today cannot stand total silence and must be eased into their relaxation experience.

Although it is hard for us to slow down, the synthesis of life's tensions and contradictions requires a quiet place. Continuous doing generally flips more energy into the complications that already exist in our lives. For example, when couples are having trouble with their relationships, often the first solution is "Let's go on a holiday. We'll take a vacation, and then we'll feel better." Well, a modern vacation generally involves expending more energy, traveling long distances, doing things from morning to night, and spending money. That doesn't help. It most likely will send the oppositions that trouble you farther apart. How often do these trips result in conflict?

Overcoming Resistance to Stopping

People in the second half of life must find ways to, in the felicitous phrase of Jung, "decently go unconscious." We all require relief from the tension and burdens of ordinary consciousness, and it is natural to seek altered states. (Watch children spin in circles until they become so dizzy that they fall down. They will laugh themselves silly, get up, and do it again.) To decently go unconscious means purposefully stopping the constant droning buzz of information that floods the mind—but not by blotting out consciousness through excessive and soulless work, eating, drugs, shopping, sex, television, or other compulsive and repetitive behaviors.

Rachel came to see me for help when her life was in a shambles and she could not seem to adjust the pace. She brought her cell phone to our sessions and interrupted our conversations to take calls.

One day, exasperated, I asked how much she made per hour.

"I bill my service out at one hundred twenty dollars per hour," she said proudly.

I inquired, "Can I hire you for an hour?"

She agreed to this. I hired her for one hour and told her I wanted her to sit in a chair and not go anywhere or do anything. She did it. She wouldn't do it because she needed to, but she would do it for $120. That was the only way I could get her to stop doing and to contemplate being.

Through the quality of our attention we can step outside—transcend—our habitual patterns and gain harmony with something greater and more complete. There is a long and rich spiritual tradition by which people achieve transcendent states using prayer and meditation. Life begins to flow again. One is open to the vast potentials and possibilities of the universe.

We are so busy living that much of the time we don't question how we experience, and as a result we neglect most of what is possible for us to sense, feel, or think at any moment. But it all still exists. Paying attention is essential for expanding our consciousness.

The Doing/Being Shuffle: An Exercise

I have developed an exercise to help bring the focused awareness of being into daily activities that I call the Doing/Being shuffle.

You can do the shuffle while standing, sitting, lying down, jogging, working—just about any situation outside of operating heavy or potentially dangerous equipment (such as driving an automobile).

- Bring awareness to the content of your experience at the moment: the words someone is saying, the thoughts in your head, and the apparently solid images all around you. Doing awareness is filled with the stuff of the world. Everything looks normal, solid, and real; it has what is called object constancy. Experiencing in this way is like taking snapshots of reality, a series of fixed impressions. Do this for about thirty seconds.

- Now shuffle your awareness to being. Let your mind go loose. You can't will awareness of being; just gently unravel the knot of sharp attention that keeps you anchored in content and forms. Sense the flow of life in and around you, starting with the changing sensations in your body. Are you relaxed or restless? What small movements are occurring involuntarily?

- Go deeper. Notice the spaces between your thoughts. See if you can anticipate your next thought before it arises, then hang out in that in-between space for a bit. Observe any patterns trying to emerge. Notice your feelings and associations. Don't judge them; just observe. Odd little ideas and images float up in your mind. Watch them move. The means by which you experience the world as solid and real—your mind—is itself constantly shifting and flowing. It's like a motion picture rather than snapshots. Just watch it unfold. Do this for about thirty seconds.

• Now shuffle back to doing awareness. The content of doing may include outer or inner perceptions. It may include sights, sounds, and smells from the outside world or thoughts and commentaries that you play in your head. If you become lost in being, get back to doing mode by asking yourself: Where are my keys? What about my billfold/purse? These are cues for the modern person to become very doing focused. The edges of reality quickly become more defined because keys, billfolds, and purses are so closely associated with our identities. Your ego snaps to attention.

Try practicing the Doing/Being shuffle once or twice a day. It takes only a few minutes. If your life is too busy, then do it while standing in line somewhere instead of becoming impatient or frustrated. Try it before falling asleep at night. Like a dance in which sometimes you actively take the lead and in the next moment you follow, in the Doing/Being shuffle you intentionally alter the quality of your attention: Doing . . . being . . . doing . . . being. Learn to shift the nature of your awareness.

As noted in chapter 2, in the early decades of life we grow by projecting unrealized potentials upon others, such as heroes, mentors, and eventually romantic partners. Our task in the mature years is to gradually integrate these energies, making conscious what had been unconscious, reclaiming what is unlived yet ripe for development within us.

Jung once said, with pithy oversimplification, that in essence there are two problems in therapy: getting people into the flow of life during the first half and then getting them back out again in the second half.

As we age, it is possible and desirable to let go of projections for pulling us into life, and we can rework those habitual and constrictive patterns of thought and behavior called complexes. By honoring a still point at the center of life's turning gyre we gain capacity to experience in new ways. Symbols become increasingly important in the second half of life for connecting us directly with the powerful, invisible energies of the unconscious. Instead of reading our world only literally and existing on the surface of life, we may begin to understand that same world symbolically, brining new depth and meaning to daily experience. This is symbolic (sometimes called mythic) life, the topic for chapter 5.

Who Am I? An Exercise

For this exercise you will need to find a partner to work with you. Find a quiet, comfortable place where you will not be disturbed. Sit across from each other. Your partner is to ask you: "Who are you?" Reply with whatever comes into your mind, such as, "I am a writer, a good friend, a wife, a daughter, a mother," and so on. Your partner is to feed this back to you, repeating what he or she has heard, such as, "I understand that you are a writer, a good friend, a wife," etc. If you are like most people, you will begin by defining yourself through outer roles and aspects of your social identity. We often characterize ourselves by our occupation, our business cards, our hobbies, and our possessions.

Then your partner again asks: "Who are you?" This time respond with different answers. With more reflection you may begin to include inner qualities, such as, "I am often angry, I feel lonely, I am sad." Try switching these statements to present tense, active processes: "I have anger in me," "I have loneliness," and "There is sadness passing through me."

Once again, your partner will feed back what he or she has heard and ask once more: "Who are you?" As you continue this exercise, do your best to deepen the sense of who you are, considering universal aspects of your being, such as "I am mortal," "I suffer," "I love." Don't imitate these answers—see what spontaneously comes up in you. Your first thoughts are the best. Your partner should feed back these aspects of identity to you, and ask again: "Who are you?"

Continue this dialogue for about thirty minutes or until your ego has run out of dualistic ideas about who you are. When you get to the zero point, "I am . . ." then simply close your eyes and reside in *being*.

5

Symbolic Life:
Curing Our One-sidedness

We have seen in our story how the parentage of Castor and Pollux came about when Leda conceived children simultaneously with her husband, Tyndareus, King of Sparta, and Zeus, King of Olympus.

In another version of this myth Zeus was in pursuit of a goddess named Nemesis, a child of the primordial goddess Night. Nemesis did not wish to couple with Zeus and she fled, tormented by shame and righteous anger. She took flight through the land and over the black sea, but everywhere she went, Zeus pursued her. Then, to further her escape, the goddess began taking the shape of land creatures. When she turned herself into a swan, Zeus, too, became a swan and thereby coupled with her. Afterward she bore an egg, from which Helen and Pollux would be born. The egg was found by Leda, who hid it in a chest. On the day that Leda's own children, Castor and Clytemnestra, were born, the egg opened and Helen and Pollux also came forth. Leda claimed these children, too, as her own.

Which version of the myth is right? In both stories, Castor and Pollux are raised as the best of friends and must eventually deal with painful separation, yet still we might wonder if the details of a myth matter. To read an ancient story not as historical fact but as timeless psychological truth, we must keep reminding ourselves that it is an inner story. Myths are polyfunctional and polyvalent—that is, they may mean different things to people from diverse cultures and in various eras. Their significance also will shift at different points within one person's life. There is no body of abstract truth waiting to be discovered in mythic stories, but nonetheless there is a sophisticated enunciation of meaning and significance.

One of the things I admire about Greek myth is that the ancients had many different stories about the most important experiences of our lives. It is only by reading and considering the plurality and diversity of stories that we can come to an appreciation of the complexity and ultimate mystery of the psyche and of life.

This story, and symbolic stories like it all over the world, can be used as psychic maps to guide the human soul in its adventure toward consciousness. All of life can be read symbolically (by allowing any encounter to engage the ego, oblige its reformulation of meaning, and thereby reframe our being). In fact, it is symbolic life that allows us to move beyond the regrets, disappointments, and limitations of unlived life and thereby achieve meaning and fulfillment. Our capacity to engage mythic sensibility is what makes spiritual experiences possible. As Jesus suggested, the kingdom of heaven is spread all over the earth, and yet we do not see it. We experience greater awareness through encounters with that which we are not. If mysteries were knowable directly, they would not be mysteries.

Signs Versus Symbols

Through language we humans attempt to designate things in such a way as to convey meaning. Sometimes we use terms or images that are not strictly descriptive; for example, the many abbreviations in modern life, such as UN, UPS, LAPD. These words have their own limited meaning, if you know it, as the United Nations, United Parcel Service, and the Los Angeles Police Department. Such terms are signs.

A symbol, by contrast, has not one but many possible meanings and points beyond itself. What we call a symbol is a term, a name, or an image that in itself may be familiar to us but which through its connotation and application also points to hidden, vague, or unknown meanings. For example, the image of the cross. For Christians a cross means much more than the intersection of two lines. It has wider unconscious aspects, qualities that can never be precisely defined or fully explained. Jung pointed out that in exploring symbols, our minds are led beyond reason and logic. There are innumerable things beyond the range of rational human understanding.

The unifying power of symbols is one the deepest and most powerful secrets of human life. That power is embodied in all of the world's great religious systems, art, poetry, music, science, and culture. We have a deep and rich heritage of symbolic life, but something has gone wrong with our relationship to many of the symbols contained within our cultural traditions. Modern society has lost the power of symbolic life, though we have not escaped our need for it.

It can be useful to reclaim what is unlived in you externally, adjusting your life to express these potentials. However, often this is impractical or impossible. For example, you can only heal old wounds with a parent or a spouse who has died or have a conversation with God through inner experience. When we experience untapped potentials inwardly, on the level of symbolic life, often the experience goes deeper, is more intense, and produces more personal development. There are many realities that can *only* be taken in at the imaginal level. You can still live whatever path you haven't taken that resides in you if you consent to explore symbolic life.

Consider a few things in your life that you cannot do but feel that you must experience. Perhaps you are short and you always wanted to be tall. Maybe you always dreamed of living in a tropical paradise, but it has never been practical. Or you always wished to be thin, or pretty, or smarter, or more athletic.

Symbolic life is the only solution to such dilemmas.

In a special form of imagination you, too, can go to your unlived life and discover what it would have felt like to follow a route different from the one you chose. You can *experience* both the negative and positive sides of it. Experience is the key word here, for that which is lived through the power of imagination is an experience, and it changes us. If done in an active form, with intention and integrity, inner experiences can be psychically real. This technique is far from daydreaming, passive fantasy, or delusions of grandeur. It will require real effort on your part—time, concentration, an open mind, and a willingness to sacrifice your conscious viewpoint—to slow down processes that usually take place autonomously and virtually unnoticed within you. In chapter 6 you will be guided through specific steps for practicing this powerful technique—active imagination—which is similar to dreaming out loud.

When you allow symbolic images to arise from within, and then in your imagination you begin to talk to and interact with these inner figures, the dialogue will reveal things you never knew about yourself.

Through symbolic life you can satisfy the hunger for the path not taken without upending the life you have worked so hard to build. In many instances you will even discover that what might have been is really not so much more wonderful than the life you have—only different. But it is important that you experience it, for all the energies essential to your authentic being demand to be expressed in some way.

Pulling Back Together What Has Been Torn Asunder

The concept of symbol is nearly as powerful and difficult to define as soul. A clue to understanding is found in the etymology of the words *symbol* and *cymbal*, which are related. The dictionary describes a symbol as a word or image that represents something else by association, "especially used to evoke the experience of something invisible." *Cymbal* means "to strike together," like the percussion instrument used in an orchestra made up of two pieces of brass that are clashed together to make a composite sound. Again we will go back to the Greeks of ancient times for guidance. The root of our words *symbol* and *cymbal* is *sumballein*, which means "to throw together," and we might say that the symbolic process is putting back together that which has been torn apart, that which has been split or set aside.

It is the power of symbols that heals the oppositions of ego consciousness. Words articulate reality into fixed entities. Yet the symbol provides a very special function in human language. In nonsymbolic use of language, articulation means determination, discrimination, and delineation—a word points specifically to a particular entity. Symbols are open-ended. Symbolic language does not primarily differentiate; rather, it fuses things into one another. For example, a flower in a poem opens itself up to diverse possibilities. As the conscious mind explores a symbol, it is led to ideas that lie beyond the grasp of reason. Therefore, in relating to figures in imagination we must accept things that are not rational and that do not follow our usual mental habits.

As I have already pointed out, it is particularly interesting that humans produce symbols spontaneously. It is difficult to sit down with a pen or a brush in hand and consciously invent a symbol. When this is attempted, as in advertising or other forms of propaganda, it generally produces a sign. We all are familiar with a stop sign, that red octagon that means to put on the brakes of your car and bring it to a halt. A sign has a literal meaning that is linked to a conscious thought. A sign carries a singular message, while a symbol carries many possible meanings. Symbols live in the unconscious (even our concept of the unconscious is a symbol).

Every night in your dreams symbols arise naturally, for dreams happen and are not invented. Dreams integrate the different energies of our being utilizing symbols that seem to preexist in the unconscious. If you dream of the fruit salad you had for dinner last night, the dream is speaking of that fruit salad as a symbol, not just telling you what you already know, the dinner menu. A symbol pulls together qualities, ideas, or experiences that to the conscious mind seem separate or even contradictory.

As we have become more rational, driven, and materialistic, we have lost the power of many traditional symbols, though we have not lost our need for them. We may think that over time we have shrugged off the need for symbolic life. Eliminating irrational ways of knowing has created a vacuum. Into this void is sucked offerings of the secular world, which knows our hunger and can profit from it, or neurotic rituals of our own devising. We are not as free to choose and not choose symbolic behavior as we might think.

Neurotic Rituals Instead of Living Symbols

Instead of having a periodic holy fast—a meaningful, symbolic action that many wisdom traditions prescribe—we've become slaves to perennial diets, a low-grade ritual without connection to something deeper in the unconscious. Instead of saying a blessing or a prayer when crossing one of life's thresholds, we check and double-check our appearance in the mirror, twist a strand of hair, light a cigarette, or drink a cup of coffee.

We have lost contact with the symbolic depths to a great extent. But the power of symbols and symbolic sensibility to daily life is still there. If you observe your own naturally occurring symbols and relate to them through simple rituals tailor-made for your situation, then much of the old power of symbolic life is experienced again.

Here is a concrete example to help set the principle of symbolic life in your mind. I have a physical handicap as a result of a childhood accident. When your body has been broken in an obvious physical way, there are limitations, potentials that clearly are extinguished. In my case, I cannot run. Losing, or not developing, any of our capacities creates a quantity of unlived life. To continue with this example, every person has running built in, but when that ability is curtailed, then objectively there is nothing that can be done about it. The unlived potential goes dark.

The unlived runner in me is dangerous, as is all unlived life. It generally comes out in neurotic form. Throughout childhood I loved both ocean-going ships and athletics—yet I could never become a sailor or an athlete. The yearning to do so existed only as a noisy potential, always threatening to break into consciousness as some symptom.

Recall that symbolic life demands that you take two pieces that have been torn apart and put them back together again. What are the two pieces in this case? One is the inborn capacity to run and a sense of freedom that is associated with this human expression; the other reality is the loss of the ability to run. Here is a contradiction. I chose to develop other talents, such as music and writing, while sailing, running, and athletics fell into my unlived life.

A Formula for Symbolic Action

It is the genius of symbol to bring these pieces together on some level that is effective for both needs. One has to run yet cannot. Left in contradiction, this clash of the opposites could easily lead to neurotic suffering.

A symbolic act, in the plainest of terms, is doing something while simultaneously not doing it. If you can learn to accomplish this—the striking together of the opposing forces—then you will free yourself in an important way.

To continue our example, how can one deal, through symbolic life, with an inability to run? Well, other activities can be substituted to sublimate the desire. Instead of becoming a sailor, you can book voyages on ships, purchase a home overlooking the ocean, enjoy stories about life at sea. I did all of those things. Instead of becoming an athlete, you could collect baseball cards, watch others play. I did those things. But somehow these substitute activities still did not really satisfy the inner need to run. I fantasized about how it would feel to run a four-minute mile, the wind rushing against my face.

What was needed was a symbolic act. To transform any collision of opposites, we must do the unlived thing while simultaneously not doing it. In other words, think symbolically, not literally.

Some years ago, at a time when this particular aspect of unlived life seemed urgent, I devised an imaginative exercise in which I had a talk with my defective legs. If anyone had come in and looked over my shoulder while this personally devised ritual was under construction, it might have been a bit embarrassing, but as a symbolic act performed in the privacy of my home it was very liberating. It is how I came to understand the power of symbolic life. I was quite surprised and eventually moved to tears by what my legs had to say about attempting to carry my desires for so many years.

Me: "Why, oh why, did this happen to me?"

Legs: "Whom should it have happened to?"

Me: "NO ONE! It's not fair."

Legs: "That's true. Life is not fair."

Me: "I didn't do anything wrong. I was just a child, only in the wrong place at the wrong time."

Legs: "That's true. Why do you hate me so?"

Me: "Because you have made me the object of scorn and ridicule. Important parts of my life have been lost. I felt shame always being chosen last or not at all in childhood games. Potential friendships with others were awkward or even curtailed. I took every rejection as due to your limitations."

Legs: "I have done my best to carry your passion through life."

Me: "I know you have . . ." (tears as the anger collapses into grief).

Legs: "Because you could not run at recess, you learned to run in other parts of your life. You also learned compassion, to accept difference. That loss gave you your first conscious experience of the heavenly realm, the inner golden world."

Me: "Yes, but something in me still yearns to run a four-minute mile."

Legs: "How can you run a four-minute mile without doing so in the outer world?"

Me: "What???"

This conversation then stalled, and I had to come back to it several times. Then an image came to me. It seemed ridiculous, but there it was. I devised a ritual with two toothpicks moving across a cutting board. As I did this, I allowed myself to imagine the wind rushing against my face and the grasshoppers jumping out of the way as I tore across an open field that once existed near my childhood home. I experienced, on a symbolic level, the freedom of running, something I could never experience in my outer life. This was one of my first meager attempts at devising a symbolic act.

Here is another example. A friend recently was complaining about the burdens of fatherhood. For more than a decade he and his wife had loved to travel. They enjoyed trips to cultural centers such as Paris to take in galleries and museums, and they enriched their intimacy over long dinners at fine restaurants. Two years ago they had their first child, and everything was turned upside down. Now a second child is on the way.

"I can't have my old life back," my friend acknowledged. We talked about his hunger for solitude, culture, and quiet intimacy with his wife. How could he address these needs through symbolic acts? Several weeks later I was delighted to learn that during a "mandatory" family Thanksgiving with the in-laws he had found time to take two excursions: a forty-five-minute walk in a nearby wood alone with his wife while grandparents watched the baby; a detour on the drive home to explore some galleries and antique shops. "I could breathe some freedom again and was less resentful," he said.

Now consider for a moment a few things in *your* life that you cannot do but feel that you must do. Perhaps you are pear shaped and always wanted to be thin. It could be that you are bored with your partner. Or perhaps you want something else. Maybe you are stuck with taking care of aging or ill parents when you really want to take off and see the world. What is unlived yet urgent in you? How is it expressed in neurotic patterns that play out in your life?

Looking for Love in All the Wrong Places

Here is another example. Suppose you fall in love with someone outside of your existing relationship. You feel a genuine attraction; whether it is right and moral, it still comes from somewhere. As noted earlier, God made you with erotic desires; this is a reality of natural life, a strong natural drive, but we live in a civilized world that says we must not tear apart other people's lives. What do you do?

There is a healthy alternative that can produce a real experience: finding a place for this desire in your life. Do not act it out unconsciously by having an affair; that is falling victim to your unlived life. Instead, consider how this passion is missing in your life and what is the hunger beneath it?

A woman I know named Courtney was faced with such a dilemma. When she came to see me, she was tied in knots. We discovered that there was a part of her that deeply resented always being nice, dutiful, and conventional. Courtney had married into a proper but somewhat dull and predictable family and settled down to domesticity in a small town. A neighbor, a college professor who ran study-abroad programs in India, caught her eye. He was worldly, intense, dashing, and spiritual—qualities that were missing from Courtney's life.

As I have said before, when you choose one thing, you always "unchoose" something else. The unchosen thing is what causes the trouble. If you don't do something with the unchosen, it will set up a minor infection somewhere in the unconscious and later take its revenge on you. Courtney had chosen a conventional life, but this did not eliminate her need for those qualities exemplified in the man who moved in down the street.

Apply the oversimplified but very useful general principle: *How can I do it* (express the unlived life) *while simultaneously not doing it?*

If you fall in love with your neighbor's husband, you cannot live out a passionate relationship directly without causing severe damage to those around you. The alternative seems to be to repress your desire, pretending that it is not there. But neither is satisfactory. You end up caught between two equally unhappy choices.

If you work with this stuck place in the psyche instead of reacting unconsciously, you can use it to become more whole. Your first step is to figure out what makes this man shine for you. Make a list of what seems so special about him. Perhaps he appears confident, sexy, worldly, or spiritual, or he is a "bad boy." Then you should also realize that to some extent these are qualities that are underdeveloped or unlived in you. You must find a way to relate to these qualities in yourself. To act out these attributes by asking a lover to carry them for you or by pursuing them at the wrong level is a tragedy and the cause of much hurt and pain in the world. The qualities that shine in others are your own potentials ripe for development. You must look for ways to honor and nurture such unlived life in a symbolic way.

For example, if you are drawn to a "bad boy," it is probably a sign that you are too diligent and dutiful in your life. Perhaps you try so hard to be good that the other side needs to be heard to balance your life. (This is a frequent problem for pastors, politicians, families of prominent people, and anyone who feels they must appear as all "good." One day their "bad" side is acted out in some unconscious manner.)

How could you break the rules a bit, be more spontaneous, own some of these "bad" qualities in yourself? How is it you became undernourished in this quality? Are there core beliefs that keep you from expressing what is unlived? To individuate in the second half of life you need to fill in the missing pieces of your personality so you can become more aware and more whole. The

Jungian term *shadow* for our purposes refers to everything in an individual that is unconscious. We could say that unlived life is that portion of the shadow that can and should be incorporated into our personalities. We have qualities and energies in us that are persistent in seeking incarnation.

The more invested and rigid you are about clinging to your conscious positions, the more vulnerable you will be to invasions of the shadow. The repressed energy then shows up as a sudden love affair, an embarrassing fit of rage, or other indiscretions. Unlived life will find its way out, whether in unconscious acts, projections upon others, psychological disturbances, such as anxiety or depression, or as somatic illness.

Does this mean that you have to be as destructive as you are creative, as dark as you are light? Yes, but you have some control over how or where you will pay the dark price.

When "Just Saying No" Doesn't Work

Despite the moral imperatives that we learn as children, sometimes it's not enough to just say "I won't do it" to banish all thought of a forbidden thing. This creates inner conflict. Who knows how much physical illness is the battleground of unlived life. You may well get a nervous stomach, back pain, headaches, or some other type of ailment when you try to practice a moralistic "just say no" policy.

It is a fact that some qualities in our unlived life are not admirable or civil. For example, I have a destructive streak in me, as does everyone. Our destructive qualities can be seen at sporting events in which the crowd expects and even cheers for carnage on the playing field, the boxing arena, or the ice rink. People line up to watch high-rise buildings being taken down in powerful explosions. We are in awe at the destructive potential of tidal waves and hurricanes and watch the terrible news reports more than once.

I try to be conscious and not act out my destructive streak in the world. Destructiveness is part of my unlived life, a part that I would prefer not to claim, but at times it breaks into my conscious life anyway. It particularly happens under stress. To deal with these energies, I must find something symbolic that can express this destructiveness.

Fortunately, we have a choice of levels by which we can realize unlived life. Start small with some humble experiments. For example, for that destructive streak I might smash milk cartons for recycling, aggressively rake the leaves, throw an ice cube against a brick wall, strike a punching bag as part of my daily exercise. These activities may seem silly or trivial, but you must begin somewhere. Maybe I need to tear apart a manuscript, showing no mercy as I slash through the flabby thinking expressed there. Or perhaps I need to cut through some illusion that I cling to in order to see clearly.

Once I counseled a woman who confessed to me that she had a problem with promiscuity. She enjoyed seducing men to gain power. She tearfully admitted that she had never felt emotional intimacy with any man, seldom had an orgasm, and experienced disgust as soon as the sex act was completed. "I will be alone with a man, and I see the opportunity. With just the right word or gesture I can turn his attention, and the seduction has begun," she said. "At some level it is like a game that I cannot stop playing."

What was she to do?

It is not enough just to think about a symbolic act. That will not satisfy compulsions or your unlived life. To be effective, the solution requires activity. In the case of the seductress, I asked her to write letters to each of the men she had seduced but not to mail them. In each letter she would explain consciously her feelings, motives, and intentions. She did this as a homespun ritual of contrition, brought the letters to me, and read them aloud with great emotion in one of our sessions. With some of the letters she cried. With others she expressed rage. She created a symbolic ritual. In the process, my client realized she had never really experienced true intimacy because she feared vulnerability.

After that day, whenever she felt the urge to act out, she would first write a letter, thereby making the unconscious conscious.

I have provided examples, but there is no simple recipe. A ritual must be tailor-made to your situation. Every morning for years a friend named Jack would go outside and talk things over with a tree in his backyard while circumambulating it. That tree seemed to provide wise counsel for Jack with whatever problems he was dealing with. For another person a symbolic ritual with a tree may mean nothing. She will have to devise her own meaningful action.

Religious traditions are rich in customs and ceremonies for meeting anything that might befall a person. There are rituals to help carry us over a threshold during life transitions such as birth, becoming an adult, marriage, and death. For some people the prescribed rituals still work effectively. Sometimes you can modify a religious ritual to meet your own requirements and thereby devise the medicine (ceremony) that is exactly right for your particular ailment—this is the highest form of creativity.

The Hunger for Symbolic Life

Jung, writing in the 1950s, could see that people in the West were increasingly living without a symbolic life. "Only the symbolic life can express the need of the soul—the daily need of the soul, mind you! And because people have no such thing, they can never step out of this awful, grinding, banal life in which they are 'nothing but,' " he wrote. Jung was angered by fellow scientists who were sold on the materialism of our time, those who insisted that humans are nothing but conditioned responses or socially constructed roles or that life is nothing but chance mutations and survival of the fittest.

When it was feasible, Jung would refer patients back to the religion of their upbringing to help deal with neurotic problems. He understood the malaise in the soul of modern life and that the great religious systems have historically provided the images and community to support symbolic sensibility. However, when a religious institution no longer contains satisfactory answers, then we are forced to go on "the quest," utilizing symbols that arise from our own unconscious.

The term *quest* may call to mind a pilgrimage or some type of spiritual journey and, indeed, this relates to what was once known as a religious crisis. The quest involves listening to your interior intelligence, taking it seriously, staying true to it, and approaching it with a religious attitude. In Jungian psychology this quest is called individuation—discovering the uniqueness of you, finding your purpose and meaning. It relates to wholeness, not some indiscriminate wholeness but rather your particular relationship to everything else. You become more whole by working through the specificity of your life, not by trying to evade or rise above the particulars of your life.

"In spite of the fact that most people don't know why the body needs salt," Jung wrote, "everyone demands it nonetheless due to an instinctive need. It is the same with the things of the psyche." Since time immemorial people have needed to believe that each life is directed to a purpose and that death is only a transition. Such religious truths can never be proven, yet they are communicated across all cultures at all times via symbolic representation.

When we learn to read our lives symbolically rather than literally, new vistas open to us. This world, the world of ordinary life, once again becomes ensouled, mysteriously interconnected, meaningful, and fascinating.

An Aging Don Juan

Sexuality is a vast and fertile field of unlived life (pornography is one of the largest enterprises on the Internet). Perhaps we struggle so with this energy field because it cuts across all aspects of our being—physical, emotional, and spiritual. An aging Don Juan, Stewart came to my consulting room and told me with great pride that he had never worked a day in his life, and that his chief purpose was to have sex as often as possible with as many different people as possible, though he acknowledged, with a smirk, that this activity was senseless and he found no satisfaction in it. At the age of forty-six, Stewart was still on a course appropriate to an adolescent. He spent several hours each day perusing erotica and corresponding with women on the Internet. His face actually changed as he recounted his sexual exploits to me; it took on the form of a mischievous, rebellious teenager who was getting away with something. He lived on a trust fund account and was drunk with freedom. He wanted no constraint on his free will, though he knew that pushing the extremes was not making his life happy or meaningful. In truth, he was not free at all—he constantly was acting out of compulsion. For a Don Juan, several women are less than one. He idealizes each partner, perceives her imperfections, and then quickly moves on to another conquest, never experiencing true intimacy with anyone.

I could see that I couldn't lecture him about morality. Stewart had heard "just say no" and various forms of religious preaching plenty of times, and it did no good. I did not want to be one more parent for him to rebel against.

"This sexual energy in you needs to be redeemed," I said. "How can you express this energy without literally 'doing it'?"

The smirk came off his face for a moment.

I asked Stewart if he knew that the average American male has at least twenty million sperm cells per milliliter of semen and that these cells are constantly being produced.

"That's me," he said, brushing the hair back from his forehead. At least I had gained his attention.

"Each of these is demanding expression," I continued. "At best, at some point a man may decide to have a handful of children, but all the other sperm cells would continue to scream at him like a chorus in Hades."

It was a pretty compelling allusion. Then I asked him how he could honor that creative urge, "screw his brains out," as he called it, while simultaneously not doing it.

He went blank, as most people do, when you ask how they might live something symbolically instead of acting it out literally. It took several weeks, but each time I saw Stewart I held my ground. I refused to let him off the hook. "How can you do it while not doing it?" I kept asking.

Eventually Stewart came back with a notebook. Inside were a series of pen and ink drawings of erotic subjects, executed with remarkable skill. We discovered that Stewart had a hidden, undeveloped talent as an artist. It began with a few sketches, but these evolved into portraits, and then still-life drawings and paintings of people, animals, and plants. He discovered his place in culture. Today Stewart is successful, teaching art and selling his art at galleries. His life found its meaning, and he no longer has to unconsciously act out his creative urges in only one arena of life.

Everything in Your Psyche Belongs Somewhere

There is nothing in the psyche that doesn't belong, though it may be expressed in a clumsy way or at an inappropriate time. The key is getting things on the correct level. The more our potentials can be honored in some way, the more whole and satisfying our lives become. To redeem unlived life we need to change the question from "What should I do to get rid of this wrong thing in me?" to "Why is the right thing in the wrong place?"

For example, that destructive streak in me is very useful; it mobilizes a lot of energy. The tendency to split life into good or bad is a major obstacle to accepting and utilizing the potentials in our unlived life. If we have the courage to look with an open mind at the qualities that have been suppressed, we will find that they can be positive strengths if applied on the appropriate level.

It takes courage to go to the "bad" side, to acknowledge it as part of oneself, and to consider that it could have a role to play in one's life. It takes honesty and humility to look directly at the fragmentation of our desires and urges. One side seems to argue "yes," while another side vehemently says "no."

I once had a client, Vickie, a highly rational engineer. Vickie was having a crisis of meaning, but she despised religion. It soon became clear that she wouldn't take anyone or anything as an authority. I asked about her religious upbringing, which was Protestant, and she ridiculed it. I told her that I accepted her negation of religion, but also informed her that she would have to find something meaningful or life would eat her up. Life is simply too hard at times without connection to something greater than one's personal will. "Why don't you invent a new religion?" I suggested. That caught her imagination for weeks. We worked on what was true for her.

Vickie utilized her scientific training for vocabulary. Then one week she came to our appointment completely flattened out and overwhelmed. "I have discovered something, but it is Christianity with a new terminology," she admitted. That was a great moment for her. Vickie saw that evolutionary theory, a scientific approach to life, was based upon nature being creative. She could not tolerate the word *God*, so she substituted *energy* to think about creation. As she read about quantum physics, she soon started sounding like a mystic.

Vickie found out that her "new" world was connected to the old world. Evolution is a mystical word for some people; it has meaning and structure and it's one way of talking about mystery. Vickie's life then began to cohere as meaningful and purposeful as she saw that human life was connected to something grand and mysterious. She found a path into symbolic life.

The Living Symbol: An Exercise

What are the unlived qualities in *your* life that you cannot express? Apply this oversimplified but very useful general principle: How can I do it (express the unlived life) while simultaneously not doing it?

To create a ritual/symbolic act, follow these four simple steps:

• Consciously recognize the conflict or tension in your life.

• Let the tension of doing and not doing build inside you. It needs to incubate in your dreams, imagination, and creativity without being acted out.

• Ask yourself, "What is really needed in this situation? What is unlived in my life that is required for my life to be more complete and whole? What could I do that is different, new, and unexpected?"

- Immerse yourself in a private, positive ritual/symbolic activity until you become one with it, until you lose your self-consciousness.

The next time you are beset by a seemingly irresolvable contradiction, recall that the lost meaning of the word *symbol* is "to clash together." Find something that represents the collision of the two impossible things in your life and hold these oppositions in your mind without immediately jumping to claim one as the "good." Surprising things will happen if you wait patiently. Ask yourself: "How can I do this thing while simultaneously not doing it?" A solution will come if you open to symbolic life.

6

Active Imagination: Talking Back to Ourselves

Do I contradict myself?

Very well then I contradict myself,

I am large, I contain multitudes.[17]

—WALT WHITMAN, "SONG OF MYSELF"

I ntentionally addressing what is unseen in us has a noble heritage: It is the vocation of poets, priests, artists, and seers. Active imagination consists of deliberately talking to yourself or, more precisely, talking to unlived aspects of yourself to alter the invisible patterns that shape your experience.

In active imagination you observe the images and voices that rise up from your unconscious and create a dialogue with them. You examine their premises and intentions. This is the most powerful way to deal with the complexes discussed in chapter 3. Once you have learned to observe your inner patterns so they do not just reflexively have their way in your life, you can set up a dialogue to modify them. You must ask yourself: "Who or what in me speaks for this?" Personify and then argue with your complexes. Unlike dreams or passive fantasies, which go nowhere when left unnoticed and untended, the ego actually takes part in the conversation—conscious participation is what makes this technique *active* and powerful.

Most of us need a disciplined practice, such as prayer or meditation, to keep our lives in balance. Active imagination is a modern form of connecting with the unseen forces that influence our lives. In fact, there is only one possible way of beginning our discussion of this discipline, and that is to quote Scripture: "Take the shoes from off thy feet, for the ground upon which thou is about to step is holy." This practice is closely related to the religious life. I know of no closer communication with God than tending to unlived life through active imagination and our dreams. Numerous passages of biblical text attest to this fact, but until recently we seem to have forgotten their truth.

Active imagination is a new form of prayer—giving careful consideration to numinous powers. Recall that the word *numinous* refers to a spiritual state of mind or a direct experience of the sacred evoking a sense of mystery and awe. Humankind has used a type of contemplation similar to active imagination since the dawn of history as a way of learning to know our gods. As Coleman Barks informs us, in the Sufi tradition there are three ways of relating to mystery: There is prayer, and a step up from that is meditation. An even closer approach is what they call conversation. *Sobbet* is the Sufi word for "the exchange," which "could also be considered a form of friendship."[18]

When the Greeks of the ancient world sought divine guidance, they stepped up to a physical representation of a god. They offered a prayer into the ear so that the god would hear. Then the petitioner stared at the divine image until the figure nodded his head or opened or shut his eyes or answered in some other way. Sacrificial offerings were also left for the divine in the form of human food; to the gods above pastry, sacrificial cakes, fruits, and wine were offered, and to the nether gods cakes of honey and, as a drink, a mixture of milk, honey, and water. Incense was added as a subsidiary offering with most sacrifices, which could include a goat, a cock, or cattle. Great banquets to honor the gods were well known to the Greeks.

In active imagination we are emulating this ancient custom. The ancients were on speaking terms with their inner figures, while we modern people think we are more sophisticated and so instead suffer from complexes and neuroses. The ancient statues, oracles, holy relics, and sacred spaces served as reference points for energies that exist in the unconscious of the person seeking guidance. What are your reference points? Active imagination is a method for exploring the unknown "other," whether we think of this other as an outside divinity or an inner psychological experience.

Today we neglect our symbolic life. We speak disparagingly of it, though it is infinitely well worth listening to. If a patient comes to my consulting room with a psychological problem, and I can convince him or her to spend half an hour a day consciously practicing inner dialogue, it is virtually guaranteed that that person will gain significant relief from the afflicting ailment.

Active imagination is the best homework you can do to reclaim your unlived life, and much of it can be accomplished by yourself. In fact, for the most part, it is a solitary occupation. It is, however, an exercise requiring discipline. If you engage in this art regularly—and it is more of an art than it is a science—there are great riches in store for you. When done correctly, this practice pulls together the different parts of you that have been fragmented or are in conflict.

Modern Heresy: "I" Is Singular

To accept such inner dialogue we must begin by considering a basic error, a great modern heresy that has been ingrained into us and is getting worse all the time: that "I" is singular. When one says I, for all intents and purposes, virtually everyone means a unified personality, this king of a little kingdom, this man or woman who owns this or that, is engaged in thus and so. For practical purposes it is useful to speak of "I" in the singular, as a unitary being. If I say I will meet you for lunch, a singular I will, hopefully, take it upon himself to show up for lunch. That is responsibility, but it is far from the facts. I, at least from a God's-eye perspective of wholeness and unity, is inherently multiple.[19]

It takes so much; it takes a multitude of energies and characters to make up this I. Virtually everyone hears a voice, or more accurately, several voices, in their head much of the time in the form of continuous monologues. While most of the time we don't do this out loud, the inner voices comment, speculate, judge, complain, and kibitz. They often compare the current situation to the past or rehearse possible future scenarios. When they are working well, our inner figures help us learn from the past and provide diverse viewpoints. Unfortunately, when limited and stuck they also can be a person's worst enemy, attacking and punishing, worrying, draining our vigor, keeping us caught in redundant cycles. The good news is that it is possible through active imagination to talk back and thereby challenge and even redeem the stuck places in our unlived life.

To benefit from this dialogue you will need to get over the prejudice that talking to yourself is a form of mental weakness. Some parents worry when they discover that their child has imaginary playmates. They shouldn't. Having imaginary playmates has been positively correlated with less aggression in boys and lowered anxiety and greater persistence in play for both boys and girls. Research shows that children with imaginal companions are less prone to anger, fear, and sadness.[20]

In our outer-oriented, materially focused society, imaginary is too often equated with unreal. In using the term *imaginal*, I want to undercut this real/unreal distinction and invoke a broader conception that honors the reality of the imaginal. Inner figures are very real psychically. We find imaginal dialogues across the life span: in children's play and their conversations with dolls and imaginary playmates, in adult dreams and fantasy, in prayer, in private speech and thought, and in literature and the arts. Yet, for the most part, in psychiatric practice such dialogues are not encouraged. Imagination and reason are deemed incompatible bedfellows. When still present in adults, imaginal dialogues may even be pathologized.

The Reality of Imaginal Experience

Our culture has a tremendous collective prejudice against the imagination. This is reflected in the things people say, such as, "You're just imagining things" or "It's not about anything real; I'm just making it all up." Due to the popular notion that the symbolic is fictitious, many people automatically dismiss inner experiences. They think, "I would just be talking to myself" or "I am just making this up; it's meaningless." In fact, no one makes up anything in the imagination. The images that arise there come from the unconscious. To be sure, inner experience is symbolic, but through these symbols we directly experience deeper and greater aspects of ourselves. Properly understood, symbolic activities transform psychic energies into images that the conscious mind can perceive. Because active imagination draws upon material outside of conscious awareness, it provides unrealized perspectives.

Experiences are always real, even when they do not accord with outer happenings. Unlike dreams or passive fantasies, the conscious ego actually takes part in the conversation; it is this conscious participation that makes it active and so powerful. The coming together of conscious ego and the unconscious on the imaginal plane gives us the opportunity to set up a genuine flow of communication among these different levels of awareness, and thus to learn more about who we are and who we might become as individuals.

This is the power of symbolic experience in the human psyche when it is entered into consciously: Its effect on us is just as great as physical experience would be. Its power to realign our attitudes, teach us, and change our behavior patterns is even greater than that of external events that we may pass through without noticing. All experience, when made meaningful, nourishes our humanity.

In active imagination you are not so much talking to yourself as participating in an inner drama. You begin to know and learn from aspects of yourself that you had never before consciously considered. When people wonder if such experience is "real," I can only respond that it is "realer than real." It not only has a concrete bearing on our outer existence but also connects us to forces that are suprapersonal. It touches on realities that go deeper than most local events in our daily lives. You cannot get rid of your inner figures any more than you can eliminate the need for a healthy ego, but you can facilitate relatedness rather than warfare between them.

We Talk to Ourselves
Already—Just Ineffectively

Social psychologist Erving Goffman has shown in his research[21] that, in the privacy of our bathrooms and our cars, we adults continue to talk to ourselves (even if we become embarrassed when we get caught). We kibitz our undertakings, relive a run-in with someone, speak judgmentally about our doings, and offer words of encouragement or blame in an editorial voice. We do this despite the social taboo against talking to yourself. In fact, people have dialogues running through their heads almost continuously, though we tend to take it for granted as a fish does water.

In other words, we all talk to ourselves all the time. The trouble is that for the most part these conversations remain passive. We replay old tapes and repeat the same old cognitive patterns over and over without actively engaging with them.

Unfortunately, imaginal dialogues represent a breach of the secular view of reality, which holds that our conversations are not to be with gods, angels, muses, or other unseen characters. Such self-talk contradicts the unitary concept of the self that relies on a stable identity and does not consider that our shifting moods and attitudes might suggest a multiplicity of self.

What if imaginal dialogues could flourish in your daily life side by side with abstract thought and socially directed communication? The real is not necessarily antithetical to the imaginal, and personifying these figures is not symptomatic of a primitive or immature mind. Personifying, which occurs naturally in dreams, poetry, and play, underlies thought and is reflective of the poetic nature of the psyche.

When the self-clinging ego personality lets go of its need for control and consistency, we are both entranced and alert at the same time. Sufis call this state *gana*, the annihilation of the individual selfhood so that the spirit of play can show through. Spiritual traditions are filled with procedures for achieving such states of receptiveness. Slowing the body and quieting the mind, as in meditation or repetitive activities such as chanting, dancing, and prayer, are time-honored ways of preparing oneself for creative growth. Both the world and the ego vanish until there is only the play; or rather forces that arise from the unconscious are playing us.

When I first began my explorations of unlived life, virtually every day I would find a new character, a new energy within myself, and I began to wonder: "When is this ever going to stop? How far does it go? How much am I? Where is the boundary at which it ends?" Perhaps this is why we read novels—to learn more and more about ourselves. One day it dawned on me that each human being contains *every* characteristic that any human in all of history has possessed, so that you are not only this small "I" but also you are *all*, a totality. Each of us is, on the one hand, an individual man or woman who exists in an ordinary life and is also a concentration point of the entire energy of the cosmic field. You are individual and supra individual. If you begin looking at your unlived life seriously, you will find a multitude of impulses and characters seeking expression in your life; you may never need to read another novel again—you will come to realize that you are a walking novel. And every one of those characters is a part of "I."

What is more, every one of those potentials rising up in you is valuable, and many need to be expressed in some way. Becoming whole is a game in which you get rid of nothing; you cannot do without these diverse energies any more than you can do without one of the physical organs that make up your body. You need to draw upon everything that is available to you.

Encountering Our Dark Side

Once you make this shift of perspective, you are in an interesting dilemma, because some of the characteristics that you discover in yourself simply won't do in polite society. For example, it costs me considerable embarrassment to admit it, but it is true: There is an undeniable greedy streak in me. What a painful recognition, but there is no way of getting around it. It is born and bred in me just as the color of my hair is and the fact that my ears take a particular shape. The only comfort is that I'm not the only one with a greedy streak, but that doesn't remove *my* responsibility for dealing with *my* greedy streak, and this is painful to me.

A greedy streak may show up as trying to hoard or hang on to material objects, wanting to possess people, or clinging to a feeling or experience after it has passed. Eating too much (gluttony) is a form of greed. Fortunately, I am also an idealist. I am a warm, friendly person. I am deeply related to my friends. As a result, I consciously choose not to land my greedy streak on the people I care about—if I can help it. It is too painful for them and for me, so I do my best not to let it out. But where does it go?

I can't get rid of this energy; there is no way. I can put on contact lenses to make my eyes look different, but they will still be the same color as the day I was born. Anyone who is around me long enough will see the true color of my eyes and eventually they will also see my greedy quality. It is part of who I am. It comes out when I am tired, overwhelmed, beaten down by the demands of life, or overcome by the foibles and suffering of earthly existence. After years of working on it, I am doing much better with this bit of unlived life in me, but it still escapes on occasion, and then I am acutely embarrassed.

Active imagination is a very useful way of coping with the difficult and embarrassing aspects of your personality, such as greed, cruelty, rage, envy, jealousy, lust, and avarice. The so-called seven deadly sins are in all of us, and when denied they are projected upon our neighbors or they break through in moments of lowered consciousness. You may begin with any mood and consider: What is the image that lies behind the emotion? When the psychic energy becomes infused with image, then it is available to consciousness.

It is not only our dark qualities that are discovered through honest dialogue with the underworld. As mentioned earlier, some of our very best characteristics, the gold in our personality, are the most difficult of all for most of us to cope with. It is often our noblest energies, such as our capacity for tenderness, love, generosity, and holiness, that are hidden most assiduously, and these energies turn out to be equally difficult to express in our outer life. For example, you simply cannot go up to someone you see on the street for the first time and say, "There is something about you that is enchanting, and I love you." It doesn't work. It is frowned upon by our society, and it would create havoc. And yet that capacity for love is one of the finest characteristics in the potentials of any human being.

Inner work provides a means to live out the gold as well as the dark—all those unlived potentials that have not found an adequate place in the practical, everyday affairs of our lives.

So we can see that active imagination involves taking aspects of your unlived life and setting up a private dialogue. In this way you can live the whole of your life without violating the cultural and social rules that hold civilized life together.

"I'm Just Making This Up"

Concerning his technique of active imagination, Jung wrote, "It has been said that both doctor and patient are indulging in mere fantasy-spinning. This objection is no counter-argument. I have no small opinion of fantasy . . . the creative activity of imagination frees man from his bondage to the 'nothing but' and raises him to the status of one who plays. As Schiller says, man is completely human only when he is at play. My aim is to bring about a psychic state in which my patient begins to experiment with his own nature—a state of fluidity, change, and growth where nothing is eternally fixed and hopelessly petrified."[22]

When you work with imaginal dialogues for a period of time you will begin to find that there isn't anyplace where you are not affected by your unlived life; it's just that normally we dismiss such encounters as "only" moods, or chance, or accidents, or other people trying to impose their will on us.

The "other" is there at all times; it is seeking interaction with you. If the other is not a surprise to you, it is not very other. Most of us have enough pursuing us that we don't need to go chasing after our unlived life—It shows up on a daily basis. The inner characters, however, take on different forms for each person.

Getting to Know Your Inner Figures

Jung once said that everything that is now accepted as doctrine in his psychology came out of active imagination with an inner spirit guide that he called Philemon (the name of an early Christian martyr). Naming these inner energies and relating to them as you would a figure on the outside are key to the practice of active imagination.

During my early training as an analyst I learned of this and immediately set about trying to contact my own inner spirit guide. I soon grew discouraged, as nothing was progressing. I sulked for a few months, thinking I wasn't good enough to do real inner work.

Then one day it dawned on me that I had a patron saint, St. Phillip of Nary. I applied some energy and did a bit of research at the library. I learned that St. Phillip was an Italian saint from the seventeenth century. Then, in an active imagination session, in my most reverential voice and language I asked if St. Phillip would condescend to talk with someone as lowly as me. The reply came rushing out of my pen and across the page of my journal: "I've been waiting for you for years; what took you so long? And I have a few things to tell you." I found from that leap of faith that there was a force of some kind in me that was concerned with my spiritual life.

For active imagination to be effective, full regard for the autonomy and idiosyncrasies of our inner figures is essential. You must be ready to let your unlived life be what it is rather than force it into your conscious notions of how it *ought* to be. Also, as in outer relationships, if you make promises to your inner figures, you have an ethical obligation to keep them. And just as in outer reality, if you are motivated solely to gain power over your partner(s), you are likely to end up losing the relationship.

Conversely, the unconscious must not be allowed to have its way unchecked by the values and obligations of consciousness. If the ego does not participate in this technique, the unconscious runs off on its own in the old patterns, unchecked and unredeemed. Then there is no relationship, and nothing is gained.

Part shadow/part gold, part evil/part divine, and part good/part bad—it's an incredible story inside each of us. The central aim of active imagination is to relieve the neurotic pressure of these unlived things and the anxiety of choice, and transfer it to the level where it really belongs, the celestial dialogue of the pairs of opposites, the song of heaven.

Getting Started: Letting Go of the Conscious Cramp

There are rules for this inner dialogue. First, it must be a true meeting of equals. You and the unlived potentials in you must relate back and forth with integrity. If it were a courtroom in the outer world, the judge would want to hear from both sides, however long it might take.

Second, it is highly useful to address the energies or qualities of the inner world as characters—to personify them. Approach them just as you would another person in your outer life. Provide them all the courtesy you can and give them half the authority in the dialogue. Notice I did not say to give them half the authority *in your life*, because it's likely this would be too disruptive and create too much damage, but half the authority in this private dialogue is acceptable. In active imagination, even one's greedy streak can have equal time.

Many like to conduct active imagination sessions at their computers. Once I got going, I learned to type very fast on a manual typewriter trying to keep up with the interior dialogue; spelling and punctuation went to the wind. Others prefer to use a notebook for their sessions. You'll need to record the experience in some way.

The images from the unconscious need to be conjured up, and this is the hardest part for most people. Everyone has a resistance; you have to discipline yourself to get started. Often people will try a bit of it and then report back that it was nonsense because they were "just making the whole thing up." My reply is, "Fine, go on and make up some more."[23]

The initial step will require patience and concentration. In most cases your first efforts will not be encouraging. Nothing may appear for a time. The exercise must then be repeated until the cramp in the conscious mind is relaxed—in other words, until you can let things happen.

At first you may feel ridiculous. Your controlling ego is likely to observe that "nobody is there" and "even if they are there, they have nothing to say." When you are awkward and squirming around, it often means that there are a lot of energies being stirred up. Whatever image, feeling, or body sensation pops up, focus your attention on it and do not let the "bird escape" until it has explained why it appeared to you, what message it brings from the unconscious, or what it wants from you.

You may find that you think of a dozen other things you should be doing. As Jung noted, "Consciousness is forever interfering, helping, correcting and negating, never leaving the psychic processes to grow in peace, observing objectively how a fragment of fantasy develops. Nothing could be simpler, and yet right here the difficulties begin. Apparently one has no fantasy, or, yes, there's one, but it is too stupid. Dozens of good reasons are brought against it. One cannot concentrate, it is too boring, what would come of it anyway, it is 'nothing but' this or that. The conscious mind raises innumerable objections."[24]

You may start with any image. Contemplate it and carefully observe how the inner picture begins to unfold or change. Don't try to make it into something; just do nothing but observe unprompted changes that occur. Any mental picture you contemplate in this way will sooner or later change through a spontaneous association—you must carefully avoid impatient jumping from one subject to another. Hold fast to the image you have chosen and wait until it changes by itself, and if it is a speaking figure, then verbalize what you have to say and listen to what he or she has to say.

How much identity should you give to these symbolic figures? Details help make them come alive. My greedy streak is loud, rude, and crude. I have given him a name, and I could tell you the kind of clothing he wears.

Apply the Ego's Ethical Dimension

Contrary to some spiritual practices that encourage us to get rid of our egos, in Jungian psychology the ego is an essential aspect of who you are—so long as it realizes that it is not the whole of who you are. It is consciousness that understands the requirements of the world. If there is an energy in your unlived life that wants to do something, it doesn't mean you literally should just run out and do it.

It is the conscious ego, guided by a sense of ethics, that needs to set limits in order to protect the symbolic process from becoming inhuman, nihilistic, or destructive, or going off into damaging extremes. Raw nature is not inherently concerned with human values such as justice, fairness, and protection of the defenseless. The hurricane that wipes out New Orleans and the cancer that invades healthy tissue are not moral or ethical. It is human consciousness that introduces these values into nature—we thereby participate in the unfolding of divine potentials within the field of time. Since the energies that arise in active imagination are often personifications of the impersonal forces of nature, it is our conscious position that must set limits. There is no development of consciousness without ethical conflict.

Jung once told the story of a young man in analysis who dreamed that his girlfriend slid into an icy lake and was drowning. In the dream the man sat there paralyzed. Jung advised him that he could not just sit there and let the cold forces of fate kill the inner feminine. He advised the man to utilize active imagination and get something to pull the woman out of the water, build a fire, get some dry clothes for her, and save her life. This is the ethical, moral, and human thing to do. It is as much the ego's duty to bring this sense of responsibility to the energies of unlived life as it is for us to tend to these principles in the outer world.

Ethics is a principle of unity and consistency. People who behave ethically are those who make an honest effort to conform their behavior to their values. When your conduct is at odds with your essential character, it reflects a fragmentation of the personality. Shirking of ethical responsibility deprives us of wholeness.

So in dialoguing with some aspect of your unlived life you must hold to conduct that is consistent with your character. Keep your practical daily life going and keep your human relationships in good order. If we are to live within a community of any sort, then we are morally responsible for our services to the unconscious energies. Refine the demands of unlived life into something that can be dealt with symbolically and thereby integrated into an ordinary human life without destroying it.

To be able to "let things happen" is very necessary, but it becomes harmful if indulged in too long. To start, twenty to thirty minutes of this exercise is plenty. It is not useful to work on active imagination for too long—if you overdo it, you will wind up creating resistance. A little bit of concentrated inner work is enough on a given day. If you feel it is getting out of hand, it's time to quit. Respect this and take it up again the next day.

Rituals and Ceremonies

Once you have dialogued with your unlived life, the final step is to find a way to honor the relationship. You should not feel finished until you find a place and purpose in your outer life for these unlived energies. Insight into the unconscious must be converted into an ethical obligation.

Rituals and ceremonies require a physical act that is meaningful. In modern life our tendency is to make everything abstract, to use wordy discussion as a substitute for direct feeling experience. Therefore, for change to be effective we have a need to get our feelings and our bodies involved. To make your unlived life manifest means that it should in some way enter your emotions, your muscle fibers, and the very cells of your body.

It is necessary to do something physical, to incarnate the energy of unlived life, to prevent it from sinking back again into the underworld of the unconscious. You must not act out. In psychological terms, acting out means taking inner, subjective conflicts and urges and trying to live them out externally and physically. Active imagination presents opportunities for this because it draws up so much unconscious fantasy material. For example, a man who is arguing in his active imagination with an inner feminine figure must be careful he doesn't turn around and pick a similar fight with his wife immediately afterward.

Applying this final step generally does not mean living your fantasies in a literal way. More often integrating your unlived life requires symbolic expression. You can get into trouble and cause harm if you fail to make this distinction. Active imagination is not a license to act out your fantasies in their raw, literal form.

Active imagination is an ancient art, and writing certainly is not the only form it may take. There are people who dance it, some will paint or sculpt it, while others may dance or jog it. People who are more visually oriented may see and draw pictures, while verbal types may hear a voice.

I recently had an interior experience that went on for weeks. The giddy thought that came to my mind was, "You are no good. You have never really made it as a writer, and in truth you can't write at all. You have no talent. Sure, you have had books published and they even have been translated into different languages, but you never got one on the *New York Times* bestseller list." I thought about this for a bit and dismissed it with the thought, "So, who wants to be on the *New York Times* bestseller list, anyway?"

"Well, *I* do," came the reply.

All right. So I took this reply to my computer and began to work on this troublesome bit of unlived life. In working on this active imagination, I found that there was a quantity of energy in me that felt terribly inferior because I had never had a blockbuster book—the kind you see on display at the grocery store checkout or at Target and Wal-Mart—as though that was a proper measure for the success of my life. This discontented character sat growling in my unlived life.

So I imagined that I got my new book on the *New York Times* bestseller list. I even got to be interviewed on *Oprah*. Success beyond belief. At first I was luxuriating in this. I was patting myself on the back (this is all symbolic, remember), the phone never stopped ringing with people wanting to congratulate me, mail came in by the bushel with offers for speaking engagements, product endorsements, and television appearances. Lots of money followed as I continued this delicious imaginative journey. Soon my friends were name-dropping all over the place, and I was feeling like a big man as people asked for autographs. After my book achieved great success, I had to hire an assistant to keep track of all the correspondence. Soon I didn't know who was my friend and who just wanted to get close to my celebrity status. Then paparazzi were digging into my past and hounding me for photographs. My privacy was lost. I never wanted these trappings of success! This went on until I learned something new from the experience.

Active imagination produces an actual experience, a slice of reality, just as potent as if you had lived it in the outer world. Recall our discussion in chapter 4 of how complexes are created in the brain. Neural pathways are established whether you experience something externally or through a vibrant inner experience. This means we don't have to live essential experiences only on the outside—consciousness can grow and we can deal with the call of troublesome unlived life through symbolic action. In this example I found out that my long-held fantasy concerning success had drawbacks as well as advantages. Then, since it was all in active imagination, I went back and undid it. I settled on writing a book that could find its own way in the world; if it succeeded, that was fine, but I no longer have this bit of unlived experience gnawing at me and a tiresome complex telling me I am a failure.

With that experience in back of me, I feel quite differently about this bit of unlived life now. That hunger, or investment, or arrogance, or discontent—whatever it was—has been lived out in me, and I am a safer, more contented person as a result. It took a few active imagination sessions at my computer to work it out, but I count myself fortunate that this nagging illusion has been quieted in me. It is no longer a noisy potential undermining my happiness.

If you have a recurring fantasy of some kind—and who doesn't—it is pure gold to transfer that fantasy into active imagination. Fantasy is always a one-sided thing. We squeeze what pleasure we can out of a fantasy and never pay attention to the other side of it. So fantasies don't change much year after year. By contrast, the active nature of symbolic life promotes change. I set about to have the most intelligent dialogue that I am capable of.

Here is another example. I might ask my greedy streak:

Me: "Why on earth did you interject yourself at that party last night? I'm totally embarrassed at how greedy I was for attention."

And the greedy streak might say, "Well, you had been playing the saint all day long, trying to convince people you are such a nice guy and that you have never had an envious or greedy feeling, so I decided it was time for people to see who you really are."

He has a point there. After consciously working at being in service to others, or trying to be particularly good or moral, one's "dark" qualities arise as a counterbalance. In this instance my greedy streak had had enough.

Me: "If you carry on like that, I will lose the respect of all my friends. People don't want to be possessed or used. Soon no one will want to have anything to do with me if they see me as greedy."

GS: "What I said was true; you did want to be greedy. You enjoy it!"

Me: "Do you think you can go around saying the truth all the time?"

GS: "That would be honest."

Me: "Well, you can't. I won't let you. For one thing, it will push people away. We would be out on the street in no time at all. Plus, I would feel very guilty afterward."

GS: "I don't have anyplace to be in your life, and I'm sick of it."

Me: "That's why we're having this discussion. I'm trying hard to live a courteous, civilized, intelligent life, and I can't have you popping up and trying to ruin it. I won't let you."

GS: "All right, if you think you are going to jettison me and be a big wimp all the time, you have another think coming."

And so the conversation goes on until the energy is drained out of it. I find a place for my greedy streak, and the saintliness or austerity or whatever it is that I have been pushing in my outer life is balanced to a humanly sustainable level. This is symbolic dialogue.

A Diversity of Inner Characters

Note that it could just as well have been a conversation with my inner critic, my long-suffering inner victim, my rageful cynic, my frightened child, or my creative muse. Which inner voice in you wants to be heard and is causing trouble? What is the recurrent inner figure making you anxious, depressed, dissatisfied, or fearful? If you pay attention, you will begin to notice that inner commentaries are occurring all the time. Whose voices are these? What does each of them speak for, and what does each speak against? You will discover a motley crew of characters, underworld shades, energies looking for incarnation. It can be a painful experience, and at first talking back to our inner figures can feel a bit ridiculous. Some people fear that talking to themselves means they have "multiple personality" or are dangerously ill.

It's true that active imagination can get out of hand for some people. Before you even attempt this technique it is wise to have someone who knows something about it available to call upon for help, such as a pastor, therapist, or trusted friend. If you have trouble stopping and you can't rein in the inner figures, then this technique is not for you at this time. Active imagination is not appropriate for anyone who tends to get inundated with unconscious material, such as individuals diagnosed with a dissociative disorder.

This process has some inherent risk—it may change your life dramatically. The analyst Barbara Hannah once said that if your knees don't shake while you're doing active imagination, you are not really there. You might breathe hard and anxiety may increase for a time. It is a real experience.

What's the difference between a psychotic and a genius? Strength of consciousness. You must not give your life over to the unconscious. The ill person has no choice, while a healthy ego chooses to listen to the unconscious and respond to it with values, morality, and ethical obligations. It is worth noting that in dissociative identity disorder (once called multiple personality disorder) there is typically no symbolic dialogue, only sequential monologue. The person identifies with or is taken over by various characters in a sequential fashion. The ego is most often unaware of the other voices. The multiplicity of who we are as experienced in active imagination is one in which inner figures are in dialogue. The ego remains strong and is always the arbiter of values. In highly dissociative states there is an absence of reflecting ego.

Even if you have a strong, healthy ego, if such inner work becomes compulsive, you should proceed with caution. There are some people who are already too open to the unconscious and more of it just gets them into trouble, but most individuals have just the opposite problem: They can't let go enough to get out of their ruts.

You can go into active imagination with or without a set agenda. For example, if I embarrassed myself at last night's party, when I get home I can sit down in a quiet place and say, "Look, I can't live in the same body with someone who gets so greedy." That sets the agenda.

There is a way of applying this technique to bring out the best in you and guard against the worst. Much of the dialogue consists of "I say" and "he says." Once it gets rolling, it is almost as if someone turned a cinema on in the back of your head and a story starts to unfold. It may seem to go on and on, but when you bring these unlived aspects of yourself into private dialogue, your conscious position and your unlived life will begin to temper each other and each will take on some of the characteristics of the other. You can get a livable and workable synthesis out of what at first may seem discordant.

Unlike the circumstance of a vaguely remembered dream from last night, a daydream, or a passive fantasy, in active imagination you are an active participant. That is the *active* aspect of active imagination. You are not just played upon; you can and must talk back. Some of the personified energies encountered in the unconscious are divine-like, while others are not at all concerned with the social requirements of your life. It is tempting to romanticize the unconscious, but the energies found there are diverse: powerful and weak, benevolent and insidious, helpful and destructive.

As analyst Marie-Louise von Franz has said, active imagination "is a form of play, but a bloody serious one." In other words, it is important not to take every voice in the unconscious as uttering the inspired words of the Holy Spirit! The inner world is paradoxical; it has positive and negative sides. The imaginal realm is not a consistent and unerring spiritual director. Underworld images do make claims on us, but they are not to be relied upon for telling us what to do. They require a dialogue between underworld perspectives and the daylight world of ego consciousness.

As noted earlier, your inner dialogue should be recorded, written down, or typed up. This is a major protection against being overcome by a powerful force in the unconscious or turning the experience into just another passive fantasy. Writing it down also provides a record so that you can remember and digest the experience afterward.

Turning Passive Fantasy into Active Imagination

Here is one more example of how to work with active imagination in a safe, effective manner.

At one point in my life I realized that I had been entertaining myself with a South Seas Island fantasy; it was always the same and I didn't want it to be any different because it was so delicious. It had to do with escaping with a fair maiden to an island with coconut palms, sunshine, and lots of erotic entertainment. It was like playing the same movie again and again. I got considerable pleasure out of this fantasy, milking it for all I could get. Over time, the pleasure in the fantasy seemed to lose its steam, but I continued to resent that I had never made it part of my real life.

As I became more experienced at the art of inner dialogue, I could see that I had been exploiting this fantasy for years, that it had never produced any development in my character. It had become a useless repetitive compulsion without yielding any inner growth. One day I went to the inner movie and began asking some questions. The fantasy began to evolve, to move, to lose its static quality. It took on an interior reality it never had before. I asked the girl in my South Seas paradise what she wanted, and she began to talk back! It seems she wanted to be adored, but she also wanted her freedom. She told me she was tired of sitting around the beach; she wanted a place in my real life. I was called upon to bring more beauty, feeling, and sensuality into my outer life.

Transferring fantasy, which is passive and repetitive, into active imagination, which is always active and real in an inner sense, is one of the most rewarding things you can do.

Most of us are afraid of what might rise up in us. It may open up a big energy center that can cause real trouble in outer life. So you'll need to get into relationship with it—privately. Don't go tell your partner that you are fantasizing about wild sex with a maiden on a South Seas island. Go talk it out with your inner character first, and then work it through.

To complete the story, when I made the South Seas fantasy active it took on new dimensions. First I discovered mosquitoes on the island, then the rainy season became apparent, and eventually the fair maiden became pregnant! The active imagination moved the old stuck pattern by bringing a bit of reality to it. And then I could let go of it. That bit of unlived life was integrated. No more envy or regret in this small corner of the psyche.

Talking It Over with Yourself: Exercises

Any human ability atrophies when it is not used. Your imaginative capacities, like your physical muscles, may require a bit of exercise to get back into optimal shape. The following exercises, derived from a therapeutic practice called psychosynthesis,[25] can be practiced at any time.

Close your eyes and visualize a pen slowly writing your name on a blackboard. Now try visualizing some different shapes: a triangle, then a square, and then a circle. Now visualize the face of a loved one. Next hold in your mind's eye the image of a favorite place you have visited in nature.

Next, imagine touching, one at a time: the rough surface of concrete, a feather, the cool water of a mountain stream, a silk scarf.

In your imagination, experience the taste, temperature, and texture of: ice cream, a raisin, a peanut, a ripe peach, and a chili pepper.

Now imagine that you smell: a rose, fresh cookies, an ocean breeze, popcorn.

Then, with your eyes closed, imagine you can hear: someone calling your name, rain on the roof, an ambulance siren, people talking in a restaurant, a tiny bell.

Once you have strengthened your imaginal skills a bit, begin engaging some of the inner figures that exist within you. Choose a controversial subject and ask yourself what you think or feel about it. Do this by yourself in the quiet of your room. Then just listen to see if some other energy system in you has another opinion. Allow it to just arise. Now create a dialogue among these different aspects of yourself. Put some energy into the argument, even exaggerating the points of view. Do this until the energy drains out of the dialogue.

Continue to practice this with some other topics. Choose an inner figure you are already familiar with, such as your editorializing critic. Engage it in a conversation. Talk back to it. Just observe the play of different points of view, allowing the dialogue to broaden your perspective.

Don't worry that entertaining contradictory energies will unseat your personality. Allowing your unlived potentials to become conscious will actually increase your integration. Through active imagination your lived and unlived qualities can become synergistic rather than antagonistic with each other.

7

Dreaming Our Dreams On

S ince ancient times people have pondered the meaning of dreams. These visitors of the night were highly valued by the ancient Greeks, as it was believed that dreams could help guide the future and offer information from the other side to help cure illness.

Asklepios, a priest and healer who is believed to have lived in the time of Castor and Pollux, wandered the countryside healing people through sacred mantras, music, dance, herbs, and dreams. His services were free, but a gift or sacrifice was expected in exchange for a cure. It was said that Asklepios became so united with the life principle that he could recall the dead from the underworld. It greatly concerned Hades to be slighted by a mere mortal and have interference with the shades that were under his domain. Hades convinced his brother Zeus that Asklepios must die, but another powerful god, Apollo, begged for mercy, and so it was that Asklepios, like Castor and Pollux, ascended to the stars to become a god, the patron of healing and medicine.

For centuries thereafter people visited the healing temples of Asklepios, where they fasted, took ritual baths, meditated, prayed, and then retreated to the abaton, the innermost sanctuary. There they slept, in a manner that was similar to being entombed in a low place, and there they waited for a healing dream. There was no guarantee, and not everyone was cured, but a sacred dream could change lives.

Merging Dreams and Active Imagination

Today dreams are just as relevant, though we have lost the art of healing with dreams. In his early work, Jung spoke of active imagination and dream analysis as two therapeutic techniques, but in later life he wrote that his dream method was based on active imagination. In the deepest sense, symbolic work (whether in the waking dreams of active imagination or the dreams that occur during sleep) becomes more than a technique; it expresses the inner-directed symbolic attitude that is at the core of psychological development.

So when it is asked, What is a dream? I answer, A dream is one of nature's creations, a spontaneous, undisguised expression of the life force that flows in and through us. It is the intersection of the daylight world and the underworld, calling attention to what is unlived yet still urgent in us. Why pay attention to dreams? For many reasons: They are enormously helpful for loosening up the knots in our lives caused by complexes. They provide a bountiful source of creativity, renewal, strength, and wisdom. They are a direct portal to what is ripe for consciousness. The images engaged within dreams are numinous (sacred space with a divine connection), for at the core of our dream images is an archetypal energy. In dreams daemons, heroes, and gods visit us shaped like people and events from the past week.

Perhaps the most important reason for paying attention to your dreams is that they humble and relativize consciousness. Dreams reframe the ego's perspective, denying its fantasies of omnipotence and enlarging our vision of what is possible. By showing us a mythic underworld filled with diverse possibilities, dreams open us to the vibrant mystery of being alive.

Some people insist that they never dream. In truth, nearly everyone dreams several times during a normal night's sleep; what varies is our ability to recall the images of the dream. The most vivid dreams occur in the phase of sleep called REM sleep, which can be detected by the Rapid Eye Movement that occurs when you are dreaming. You may have noticed a dog or cat asleep with its eyes twitching beneath the eyelids. This is REM sleep, and it indicates that a dream is occurring. Adult humans spend about a quarter of their sleep time in REM, a condition in which the body is nearly paralyzed but the brain is buzzing with activity. Researchers using advanced computer technology to watch the dreaming brain have found that one of the most active areas during REM sleep is the limbic system, which controls our emotions.

Remembering Your Dreams

To improve your dream recall, start with a pen and notepad or a dream journal kept close to your bed. A voice-activated tape recorder also can be handy, as it doesn't require turning on a light to record the dream. If you wait until noon to write down that "unforgettable" dream, you are likely to find that it has disappeared like vapor before you've even finished brushing your teeth. If at first all you have is a fleeting image or an emotion, record that. If you pay attention to what is given, the next night you are likely to remember more. If you are cynical and show little interest in your dreams, you probably won't remember much. It is as if the inner dream maker returns the attitude you show to it. If you approach a dream with interest and curiosity, you will be rewarded with greater recall.

Jung, who wrote volumes about dreams, noted, "Usually a dream is a strange and disconcerting product, distinguished by qualities such as lack of logic, questionable morality, uncouth form and apparent absurdity or nonsense. People are therefore only too glad to dismiss it as stupid, meaningless and worthless."[26]

"I have no theory about dreams . . . I share all your prejudices against dream interpretation as the quintessence of uncertainty and arbitrariness. On the other hand, I know that if we meditate on a dream sufficiently long and thoroughly, if we carry it around with us and turn it over and over, something almost always comes of it . . . I must content myself wholly with the fact that the result means something to the patient and sets his life in motion again . . . for very often the standstill and disorientation arise when life has become one-sided."[27]

Dreams speak in the language of symbols, so you must learn to translate dream language, but this doesn't mean you should go out and purchase a dream dictionary. Attempting to pin a symbol down to singular meaning, such as a horse in a dream equals instincts or emotions, is not helpful. Every dream symbol is multifaceted. Like a jewel, it will reflect the light differently as we turn it about in various ways. You must interact with the dream images.

As with cinema, dance, visual arts, or poetry, each dream is multilayered and can have boundless meanings. We may never understand a dream completely from the conscious viewpoint, but the act of relating to a dream is what is most important. You can work with the images in a dream just as you would in active imagination with a complex or a mood, developing a dynamic relationship with the energies that emerge.

What Does the Dream Want?

Consider dreams as a call from the underworld, seeking not interpretation so much as incarnation in our lives. The wonderful

Spanish poet Federico García Lorca used symbols to evoke mystery and wonder. In a poem called "Casida de la rosa," he wrote:

La rosa
no buscaba la aurora:
casi eterna en su ramo,
buscaba otra cosa.

La rosa,
no buscaba ni ciencia ni sombra:
confín de carne y sueño,
buscaba otra cosa.

The rose
Was not seeking the dawn:
Almost eternal on its branch,
It looked for something else.

The rose
Sought neither science nor shade:
Bordering flesh and dream,
It looked for something else.[28]

(TRANSLATION BY JEREMY IVERSEN)

Like all great poets, Lorca utilizes symbols to open our experience. His readers are led to ask: What is this other thing, and how does this poet know the rose does not seek the dawn, or shade, or science? What is the relationship of flesh to dreams?

Here I have drawn upon the work of Jungian analyst Russell Lockhart,[29] who points out that it is the nature of the conscious mind to ask questions, interpret, and search for logic. Yet there is another voice in us that may respond to the poem on a different level, a quiet voice that simply says, "Yes!" Poetry uses language as symbol, and symbols open up our experience to wonder and creative possibilities.

In active imagination you can take any dream as a jumping-off point and then dialogue with the dream symbols. Allow the images to rise in you again as you say the dream aloud in the present tense. At the point where the dream ends, simply wait with patient expectation. Observe what happens next. Watch the images in the dream. Stick to the image; don't rush to interpret it. Only in this way can we befriend the dream, and get to know it as we would a person in outer life.

For example, rather than wondering if a snake has sexual connotations, bring attention to the qualities of the snake in your dream, such as its scales. Close your eyes and focus on those snake scales. What are their color and texture? Details are important in making the images come alive. What happens when you stop to face the snake? Reach out to touch it? In your mind's eye, allow the dream image to come alive and then let it unfold before you. See what discovers you, rather than the other way around.

Psychologist Stephen Aizenstat aptly describes this approach as *hosting* a dream rather than dissecting it. You relate to it as living entity within the ecology of the psyche. Let go of trying to find the correct interpretation of the dream. The point is not to analyze or interpret it and thereby translate it into the ego's language and desires. Focus on the "what" of the dream rather than the "why." Dreams are to be related to on their own terms; they are examples of psyche speaking to itself in its own language. This is a language of metaphor and symbol, so you need to play poetically with the images in your dreams. In this manner you can re-enter the dream experience as sacred space with a divine connection.

Suppose the author of your dreams wanted to talk about old age. He would not go and write *old age* on the blackboard. He would create a setting, such as a rocking chair, on the stage. This is the playwright's way of talking about old age. That is how a dream symbol arrives—in picture language.

Living with the images of the dream brings consciousness in contact with the irrational customs and desires of the underworld. The art of letting things happen is the key that opens the door to this realm. As already noted, the hardest part for most modern people is to let go of the grip of consciousness so the images are allowed to speak. We must give time and patience to the dream images, jumping to no conclusions.

I once had a client, Eve, who was divorced and the mother of two children. Her live-in boyfriend was a financial drain and would not commit to marriage or much of anything else. He was something of a sponge, made little effort to relate to the kids, and was not one to talk about his feelings. She could see no future with this man but was worried about her finances without him, even though he contributed little to the monthly budget. Then she had a dream:

I am on a horse named Coke; he was my father's favorite horse. We are going down a hill, and he wants to lock his legs and slide down the hill. Something is wrong with the horse. I get off. He rolls three or four feet to the bottom of the hill and then dies with his eyes open.

Eve was completely baffled by this dream. At first we tried to interpret it. She was not fond of horses. "They are too unpredictable, not to be trusted," she informed me. Rather than speculating that a horse means this or that, I asked her to recall the image of that horse and to notice what it felt like as she watched it die. As the images came back to her, they seemed to fill the room. She observed that the horse's coat was tattered and worn. That he smelled bad, like something a bit rotten. Then she noticed that the horse died voluntarily, just rolling himself up on the ground. "What wants to die?" I asked.

"I don't know," she insisted, but the images were active in her imagination now.

The following week Eve returned and announced that she had decided to kick her boyfriend out of the house. She had a follow-up dream:

I am at a wilderness ranch. I am playing near a pool when a dolphin swims up to play with me. I reach out to touch him. Then there are dolphins all around me. They want to play with my legs. At first their rough skin feels a bit odd, but I get used to it. Then I look out and see that there is a female dolphin that is ready to give birth. The male dolphins are there to protect her.

The first thing that jumped out in this dream was the flow of energy, as Eve imagined putting her feet in the cold water of the pool. Then something miraculous happened—dolphins appeared. "They are very protective. They want to help me," she said with new confidence.

After she worked with this dream in active imagination, it became clear to Eve that all she had to do was take a small risk (put her toe in the water) and tremendous growth would occur. The dream generated optimism and courage in her, as she felt that something new was being born. Indeed, a new attitude toward the masculine was being formed, as Eve considered how she had been relying upon men for qualities that were ripe to be claimed from her unlived life, qualities such as financial independence and practical capabilities such as overseeing car and home repairs. She no longer needed to ride on the back of needy dependence on the masculine, an attitude and orientation to life that began with the experience of her father. His horse, Coke (no, there was no drug use in the family), turned out to be a potent symbol of the father complex. The limitations of an old attitude needed to die. The archetypal father image serves as a prototype for our capacity to feel our own worth, self-confidence, and the capacity to carry out necessary life tasks. When we consciously or unconsciously feel inadequate to this task, this is called a negative father complex. Assumptions may originate with the biological father, but they are subsequently reinforced by other relational and cultural experiences.

Over the weeks following her dream of the dolphins, Eve changed the locks on her doors so the former boyfriend could no longer drop in unannounced. Her small business continued to grow and her financial worries quieted as she realized that she could take care of herself and her children. She developed an insatiable appetite for books and films. What was most remarkable was that Eve had always enjoyed playing pool as a hobby, though a lack of confidence held back her progress in tournaments. Recall her second dream with the new birth in the pool? Dreams often make puns with words, showing us the multidimensionality of a symbol. Well, a year after having that dream, with her newfound confidence, Eve entered and won an amateur pool championship in eight ball!

Interacting with Dream Images

If there is too much of something in your lived life, your dreams will tell you. If there is too little of something, they will inform you of this. If you are overdoing or underdoing, the dream will serve as your guide. Dreams comment on somatic conditions as well as the psyche. They can predict disease and provide cures. So you will need to put some energy into interacting with your dream symbols.

If your dream includes falling, ask of your dream image, What is falling or how am I falling? From grace? From esteem? In love?

If there is an image of flying, ask yourself, What am I flying over in my conscious attitude? Am I flying off the handle? How am I inflated? What yearns to fly in me, to grow wings and take flight? Am I flying toward or away from something? Is a transcendent perspective trying to free me in some way? Experience flight in your mind's eye and watch what happens.

People often dream of toilets. What needs recycling? Where am I wasted, overflowing, or flooded? What about my privacy? Do I need to let go of something? Imagine yourself talking in or even *to* the dream toilet. See yourself as the toilet. What is it like to get "dumped on"? Enter the dreamscape, watch the image, and observe what happens.

Dreams are marvelous at filling in the chinks in your personality, pulling you toward your destiny in small turns. Sometimes this is accomplished parenthetically. There are times when a dream doesn't have the solution; it is vague and only states a problem or reiterates a stuck point. If you relate to the images as far as the dream goes, however, it may help to set the stage for later development.

A voice within you is likely to argue that all this fuss over a dream is a waste of time. Thank it politely for offering this opinion and providing practicality to your life—and then continue to listen to your dreams with high regard.

The goal is to create an experience in the here and now rather than a dry analysis of the dream. After recording a dream, you should describe it aloud in the present tense, use "ing" words, as if it were happening NOW. This will help to "dream the dream on."

Try exploring the dream landscape,[30] concentrating on "what" rather than "why." Wait for images to fill the silent space.

Inner Work Affects the Collective Psyche

Some people, or some skeptical energy in you, will argue that tending to dreams is a fool's errand, a self-indulgent distraction from the real and urgent demands of the outer world. Your inner work inevitably affects those around you and the world as a whole. Like ripples in a pond, the energy released from making the unconscious conscious often has far-reaching implications.

I had a client who worked very hard on her dreams for six months. She hadn't told her husband that she was coming for therapy, and she paid me out of her grocery money. One day she came in angry, threw herself down in the chair, and said, "It isn't fair."

I asked, "What isn't fair?"

"I work like a dog on my dreams, and my husband, who thinks it's all a joke, derides my efforts. He seems to be happier than I am!"

That can happen. Do not succumb to the concern that devoting time to inner work is an exercise in navel gazing or narcissism. Such comments often come from family and friends who have a vested interest in our predictability and consistency. As you retrieve unlived life, it will shift the nature of relationships—conscious and unconscious—with those around you.

Jung pointed out that individuation has two aspects: In the first place it is an internal and subjective process of integration, and in the second it is an equally indispensable process of objective relation-ship. Neither can exist without the other. No individual is a single, separate being, so it follows that "individuation must lead to more intense and broader collective relationships and not to isolation."[31]

You cannot predict the direction your inner work might take, but in bringing more consciousness into the world you are assist-ing the evolution of the collective as well as yourself. The Torah says you may pray at one altar for the fire to fall and instead it falls on your neighbor's altar. If you invest in the marriage of the inner and outer worlds by putting honest energy into dreaming a dream on, all the people in your life, maybe the whole of hu-mankind, is enriched, though it may not produce the result your ego was seeking. This is a saint's task, clarifying a bit of the collective unconscious for the good of all humanity.

Once you have worked with a dream and something has moved in you, or there is some new insight concerning your habitual pat-terns, you will remember more dreams. If the dream repeats a theme, then your interior relationship to that experience is not fin-ished. The dream will usually make small variations, giving you a hint of what to do. Each dream is a step in your developmental process, and if you interact with it, the next one will be different.

There are circumstances in which dreams repeat a scene or mo-tif over and over. For example, if the person has been subject to trauma such as a war, violence, a serious accident, abuse, the death of a loved one, a natural disaster. Experiences such as these are often too far outside the bounds of our usual ability to cope and cannot be easily assimilated; as a result, they will come back as inner experience repeatedly until the person can find a safe way to integrate the dream material. A wise and experienced mentor may be needed so that the images in the dream can be assimilated in a safe manner that does not continue to retraumatize the psyche. A professional therapist can be most helpful in such situations. This applies to people who have recurring night terrors. There are experiences that shock us so badly that we can only take them in a bit at a time.

If we commit to reworking our most painful experiences, then we are less likely to pass them along as a heritage to our children or others.

In relating to a dream, always ask: Why has this visitor appeared? What do I need to learn? What am I not perceiving from my ego's current point of view? If you spend a bit of time with the dream, you will influence the underlying patterns in the psyche—even if you cannot come to a clear conclusion. The release of energy will be good for you.

Inner or Outer Reality?

In dream work seminars, I am often asked: "Is the dream commenting on my inner life or on the external situation?" For example, if I dream of a fight with my wife, does this mean that tension is building and a quarrel with her is approaching, or is the dream about being on bad terms with my inner feminine qualities? People often get confused here, because the unconscious has the habit of borrowing images from outer life and using them to symbolize dynamics that are going on inside the dreamer.

In truth, dreams are multidimensional and make no distinction between inner and outer. The imagery in a dream can and should be applied to both domains of your life. If a man is on bad terms with his inner feminine, then he is likely to fall into a mood, and a quarrel with someone on the outside is likely to follow. What happens in inner life will draw that experience to you in outer reality.

However, from a practical standpoint, in working with dreams I always look for the inner connection first. Since our culture trains us to value the outer world, people generally jump to the conclusion that dreams are commenting directly about something on the outside. If you consider a dream as a rerun of the day's events, then it will usually seem superficial and not worth troubling over. But then you will be missing some of the most important aspects of the dream.

Start by assuming that the dream is about your inner dynamics, not outer reality. For example, a man dreams of a plane crash and concludes that he had best not travel. But he could look at the plane crash as a symbol he is already involved with in some way: Something in his life is coming down in a destructive manner. Even when a dream makes some direct comment on an external situation, it is doing so in terms of the inner condition that precedes it.

The urge to take dream images literally is strong. Many people will try to use a dream as an excuse to blame the external person or to congratulate themselves on how right they are. But if you resist that temptation, you will have a better chance of understanding what bit of unlived life is calling for you to claim it.

I recall a client who came to me with a dream in which his sister drove a car too fast and subsequently crashed into a building. He feared that the dream foretold an auto accident and wanted to call his sister to warn her. I suggested that it would be more useful to start from the subjective viewpoint, with the assumption that the dream was symbolizing something in his own inner life, such as a runaway compulsion or moving too quickly with some enthusiasm that was about to get out of control. I asked him to talk to the inner image of his sister (not his literal sister), taking the dream into active imagination. What was he doing that might be out of control? This led to some insights that the dreamer had not considered.

Remember to think imaginally, not literally.

Here is another example: If you dream of a train, usually it is not about a train on the outside but some part of you that is train-like. Perhaps it is your determination, storming down the tracks. Maybe it is a runaway enthusiasm. Visualize your dream train. Feel its power. Notice the details to help the images come alive for you. How does this train sound, smell, feel? What do you experience in your body as you host this image?

Telos: Dreaming the Future

Dreams are often forward looking, teleological. The ancient Greek word *telos* relates to the pull of the future. It is a most beautiful word. Our scientific culture is so ingrained with cause and effect that we tend to want to relate to all things in such a manner. However, there also seem to be unseen forces that pull at us to accomplish certain goals.

There are dreams that foretell something about to occur outside the dreamer. For example, people will dream of disaster just before a war breaks out or someone close to them dies. The dreamer later discovers that the event actually took place in outer reality. This is rare, but it does occur.

Once you have gained some insight from the dream images, to truly benefit from symbolic work you must eventually *do* something different. Even when you have had a vivid experience interacting with dream images, your insight is most likely only from the neck up. You must then acquaint the rest of your body with it. An old rule in Catholicism is that a prayer doesn't count unless your lips move—it is not enough just to recite it in your mind. The same is true with dreams. There will be no effect if you don't put it down on paper and then do something to incarnate the images. Activate your muscles. Most people today have become so theoretical and abstract that at times they need to be reminded to engage the physical body and do something tangible.

For example, if a dream makes it clear that you feel guilty about the money you borrowed, you should go pay back the loan. Unfortunately, dreams aren't always that straightforward. Then you must be creative and devise a ceremony to honor the dream in some small way. If you are absolutely stuck, you can go out and walk around the block; just do *something*, even if it makes you feel a bit foolish.

I recall a marvelous man, a Benedictine monk, who was in analysis. He hadn't been aware of his body for thirty years. His dreams seemed to be trying to round him out, presenting parts of his life that he had neglected. He was doing his best to ignore both his dreams and my suggestions that he needed to pay attention to his physical nature. One day I lost my temper with him and told him it was not enough to have intellectual discussions about the content of his dreams; he needed to get out and do something with them.

"What would I do?" he asked with a blank look.

Exasperated, I blurted out, "Well, if you can't think of anything else, then go look at the bark on ten trees!"

He silently stood up, cleared his throat, gathered his things, and walked out. I felt I had offended the poor man, lost my composure and pushed him too far. Then, a few hours later, there was a knock on my door. He had returned. "You have no idea how interesting the bark on trees is," he said. "Some of it is rough, some smooth, some brown, some gray; it's different on the north than on the south side; insects live in some of it. You know, different trees have different smells," he said. As he awakened to the realm of the senses and his own physicality, his healing began. He started to be able to shift out of the abstract, intellectual realm in which he had lived for decades. Now whenever I see him I ask how his trees are doing, and we both laugh.

June, a woman in her late thirties, came to see me because she claimed that she could not feel anything. "Other people talk about feelings, but I have always been empty," she confessed. All of her experience was processed as thoughts in her head. She grew up in an Appalachian family with a mother who worried constantly and was frightened of the dangers outside their small and circumscribed existence. Mom warned her children that if they left home they would most certainly fall ill and maybe even die, as the world was a threatening place. My client's father was given to rages, which would terrify the children. June was the only one in the family who did leave home—she broke out, went to college, and became a pharmacist in a neighboring state, yet life felt flat to her. This is one of her dreams:

I am inside my house. Looking through a window, I see bluebirds outside. I am very excited and tell everyone in the house. I tell them not to walk near the window or they might frighten the birds. My youngest sister doesn't hear me and walks by, and I am fearful she will ruin the situation, but then my husband and I are flying with the birds. It is as if we are floating with an entire flock of bluebirds. I wonder if we will fall out of the air or keep flying.

June's feelings, like the bluebirds, were just outside the window and inviting her—spirits in flight. In response to this dream, June decided to draw the bluebirds, make up stories about them, and then talk to them. She worked hard and made slow but steady progress processing the unlived life of her family. It took considerable effort to become free of her mother's fears and let her feelings become airborne. There followed a series of dreams with threatening men. In the dreams she ran away or tried to make herself small when these figures appeared. A turning point came when, in active imagination, she was able to confront one of these dark and cruel men. Her body shook with the energy that was released when she reclaimed her power.

Remind yourself that understanding or interpreting a dream is not often the most important thing. That is the desire of the ego. The dream allows other aspects of the psyche to have a chance to speak. Energies from the underworld attempt to address us many times each day, but generally we are too busy with our conscious agendas to hear them, so they break through at night.

Aging and Death Dreams

One of the most frequent dream motifs in the second half of life involves dying. Often this will indicate that some energy system or old pattern in you is expiring; you must not conclude that your physical death is imminent. You may be at the end of a certain era in your life and some aspect of you needs to die and transform to clear the way for further development.

Here is a dream I had about three years ago:

I drive to San Francisco in my old Volkswagen Beetle. I park it. Then I forget where I have parked it and, though I can't find my car, I have to go home again. I walk till I am exhausted. I'm feeling desperate, then I find my wallet is gone; I remember a friend in San Francisco had a wallet stolen, and he ended up at a Bank of America branch, which is also my bank. He had no identification or money, not even change to phone someone for assistance. He got help when they phoned back to his branch and verified that he had an account and then gave him a couple of hundred dollars, which pleased me greatly in my dream. So in the dream I thought, "If I can just find a Bank of America, they will bail me out from this difficulty." I begin walking again. I cannot find a branch of Bank of America (though, in outer reality, there are many in San Francisco). *Finally I am completely stuck, and from that stuck or zero point I suddenly realize the basic life principle that I am exactly where I belong, that I don't really need anything, not a car, not the Bank of America. I realize this with great relief and joy.*

Later that night, a second dream:

I am in a city again, this time in a medieval setting. I'm trying to find my way out of the city to get to where I am going. Every street that I take leads me back to where I started. It is a bit like a maze. I take different turns and go though hours of searching (there was great detail in the dream that I cannot now recall), *but no matter which direction I go, I always end up at the same point. The third time I try this, still ending up where I started, is my final attempt. Exhaustion takes over, I surrender, and it comes like a revelation to me that all streets go both directions simultaneously and always take you back where you started—it seems this is the nature of reality!*

This dream expressed the condensation of months and months of preoccupation with pairs of opposites, as I struggled with a Castor and Pollux split in me. I was tired of the demands of the world, with its deteriorating cultural climate, political conflicts, and constant demands upon my energy. A part of me was ready to die, to leave the earthly world for the eternal Pollux realm on Olympus, so at one level this was a death dream. Yet at the same time I was bound to this earth by my love for those closest to me.

At the time that I had this dream I had greatly reduced my lecture schedule, and my identity was changing, as represented by the missing wallet and identification. In tending to this dream in active imagination, I struck up a conversation with the bank teller. He made it clear that not even the Bank of America could rescue me. "You are entering old age—the twilight years," the teller pointed out. "Surrender your identity from your earlier life." As the dream image instructed, I had to let go of trying to do anything about my situation and accept reality as it was. I needed to stop fighting both the inner and outer process, including the limitations, of growing old.

Only at the point of exhaustion did a revelation set in and the totally irrational conclusion was reached that this is wonderful! Was I gaining some piece of enlightenment in my declining years?

In the second dream all streets go both directions simultaneously and always take you back where you started—this is the nature of reality. This concept may be bad news from a conscious perspective, but in the dream it felt as if I had discovered the secret of heaven.

These dreams were important for me, communications from the underworld preparing me for the major life changes we all eventually face—retirement and, eventually, physical death. I have gradually realized that it is unlived life that has not been made conscious that accounts for the greatest part of the struggle and painfulness at the moment of death. If we work with our dreams to resolve what is unfinished yet urgent in us, then much of this pain can be eliminated.

My friend Jane worked as a chaplain at a Philadelphia hospital. In this role she was regularly called upon to sit at the bedside of dying men and women, offering them solace and comfort. She heard one theme repeated over and over—a sense of betrayal. "They thought that if they met the responsibilities of life, fulfilling the culturally prescribed things that we all feel compelled to follow, that somehow life would not run out before they had a chance to live it. Yet in those precious moments before death they realized there was no more time. It was too late, and they had missed some essential experiences," Jane recalled.

Imagine that right now there is no more time. Then you can begin to truly live.

When I resided in India, dead bodies could be seen daily on the street or near the ghats of the Ganges, and there was much less mystery about our inevitable dissolution of form. In modern Western culture we tend to hide death as though it is something that should not be.

Dreams concerning physical mortality often show order and unity, as though the contradictions of life are resolving themselves. For example, here is one from a client of mine, an elderly woman who had been diagnosed with cancer. She was a beautiful, sensitive, and fragile person and also an artist of some talent. At the time of this dream she had already undergone one major surgery to remove a tumor, followed by radiation treatments and then chemotherapy. This dream occurred during a time of crisis, when she realized that despite efforts to battle the cancer, it had metastasized and could no longer be contained. She was terrified. Then the following dream came:

I am walking downhill to a lake. The water in this lake is very clear. I can see all the way to the bottom. The rocks are all the same size, though they are turned in different ways. To the right, a man is swimming in the water, and he seems to want me to join him. Then, to the left, I see a beautiful unicorn. It is up to its knees in the water, and it is gorgeous. The bottom part of the unicorn is dissolving into patterns or waves, while the top is like a beautiful statue. Others are fearful of this animal, but I am not. The most intense feeling is one of clarity, as though I can look right to the bottom in this dream.

This image of the unicorn was miraculous, a gift from the unconscious, but at first the dreamer did not want to accept it. The dream promised that if she could be honest about her impending death, she would see immense beauty in it. The water is so clear she can see right to the bottom of existence—every rock is in place.

The unicorn is a mystical animal, a symbol of oneness and unity, sometimes spoken of as a Christ symbol. In this context it seemed to refer to a gathering of the pieces of this woman's life into a unity. At the time of this dream the dreamer still had unlived life, and it was torturing her. The dream seemed to indicate that if she could make this conscious, she would possess clarity, completion, and wholeness. This dream attempted to inform her what the death experience could be like; her distress was given a direct answer.

The unicorn dream was wonderfully clear. What the dreamer was afraid of actually was the glory of her life. In our next session I brought a treasure that had been given to me years earlier: a narwhal horn. Though the horn was from a sea creature, it looked remarkably like our ideal of the unicorn horn—its intricate white spirals extend twelve inches from the base to a pointed tip. I asked my client to hold it while visualizing her dream images. I believe that this woman's powerful dream symbol helped her in her passage to the next realm. In our last conversation before her death, she seemed illuminated by peace and had surrendered her fear. I shall never forget our meetings.

Dream Tending: An Exercise

If you'd like to get in the habit of remembering your dreams, try the following dream incubation.[32] Eat lightly on the evening that you plan to host an informing dream. About ninety minutes before going to bed, begin preparing yourself. Bathe in a leisurely way, holding the thought that you are cleansing body, mind, and heart. Put on a clean robe or night wear you feel relaxed in. Meditate or collect your thoughts for a period of time. Imaginatively reach out to another presence that can help you in your efforts. This could be identified as your soul, a higher power, your creative spirit, a muse, the unconscious, the higher Self, your patron saint, or a guardian angel—whatever is real and vivid for you. Ask this presence whether it would be willing to assist you in your dream tending.

Now write down a number of questions or topics that come into awareness. Choose one, or let one choose you. The topic should carry energy and have promise. Rewrite the question or issue into one clear, short sentence or phrase. Whisper it or say it aloud. Then write down the answers to the following questions:

- How is this issue significant for me now?
- What is my deepest desire concerning this issue?
- What are my fears concerning this issue?
- What is the covert payoff for keeping this issue unresolved?
- What would I be willing to give up or sacrifice to have this issue resolved?

As you begin to feel drowsy, repeat your issue or question. Go to sleep with the expectation of getting new perspectives during the night. When you awake, write down everything you remember right away, before it disappears like the night stars.

A dream is more cinematic than literary, with quick cuts, flash-backs, and simultaneity of action. When we write the images down into linear, grammatical sentences we lose much of the actual lived experience of the dream. To regain the sense of a flowing, dynamic process, after you have recorded a dream to aid your memory, try eliminating punctuation, such as commas, periods, and capital letters, in the narrative. This way when you read the dream back it will have more flow and will better invoke a living process.

Sometimes I like to think of dream images as an animal (such as a cat). They are independent creatures that do not particularly care to be analyzed, interpreted, or made to walk in straight lines. They do, however, appreciate relatedness. Perhaps it wants to have its ear scratched, to be fed, to be let out to play, or sometimes just to be admired. The same is true for your dreams. Talk to your most vibrant inner figures, and see what happens.

You might also play with the dream images by changing the nouns in your dream record to verbs, action words that are in process. For example, if I dream of an apple, I might consider: What is "apple-ing" about (i.e., what would it be like to be an apple?)? Is something in me ripe? Sour? Keeping the doctor away?

When you allow yourself to get into a living relationship with the dream images and what is happening in the scene, you will find that the meaning becomes less important. Befriend the images in your dreams, and try meeting your dreams, not with analysis but with curiosity, affection, and wonder.

8

Two Essential Archetypes for Maturity

I n our guiding myth, unity and peace are achieved when Zeus divinizes Castor. The two energies that had been separated are reunited into an essential oneness. Romans called Castor and Pollux the Twin Brethren and associated them with the principle of brotherhood and balance considered to lie at the foundation of their empire. In Egypt an analagous pair were known as Horus the Younger and Horus the Elder.

We have already seen that it takes a multitude of energies and characters to make up the "I." In this chapter we will focus on two of the archetypal forms that hold particular interest as we age: the Eternal Youth and the Wise Elder.

The Eternal Youth is uplifting, inspired, experimental, optimistic, idealistic, fun-loving, and endlessly creative. It also is irresponsible, mercurial, and hard to pin down. Eternal Youth–dominated people (whatever their chronological age) often seem possessed by an almost sublime if somewhat dreamy spiritual quality. Jung called this pattern the *Puer* (Latin for "boy") and the *Puella* ("maiden").

For many modern people under the weight of duties and responsibilities, this essential Puer energy has been all but squeezed out of them by life's later decades. Yet this irrepressible youthful quality lives within each of us, at least as a potential. Even if you are ninety, the Eternal Youth is still around in you—we hope—because this is your contact with new consciousness that is not based upon old patterns, existing rules, or written laws.

The visionary inspiration of the Eternal Youth finds its polar opposite in the earthy pragmatism of the Wise Elder (called by Jung the *Senex*, a Latin term that means "wise old man"). This is the forming energy for practical structures and systems, and its influence can be seen in our laws and institutions. Stable. Ordered. Controlled. Disciplined. These are Wise Elder qualities. Without the influence of the Wise Elder, the youthful creative energy in us has difficulty bringing ideas, visions, and aspirations into concrete reality.

Although the Eternal Youth and Wise Elder do not live easily alongside each other, both are needed to balance the human personality (and society). These are contrary aspects of an underlying reality, and wherever one polarity appears, somewhere its opposite will live as a counterpoise. The struggle between these archetypal energies is an attempt to reconcile the inevitability that they are part of the universal dilemma of how to bring divine beauty and creativity into practical earthly life, spirit into matter.

We all know people and institutions that do not age gracefully. Some trade youthful enthusiasm for what society calls responsibility and become reactionary, defensive, and stiff—cut off from the creative spirit of Eternal Youth. Far too many old people become hypochondriacs, pedants, or applauders of the past as substitutes for the broadening of the self that is called for in the second half of life. There is an instinctive Puer energy in us that needs to be recalled and cultivated as we age. Without the ongoing presence of the Eternal Youth, we become morally rigid, dogmatic, judgmental, and authoritarian; we are bound to law, structure, and safety.

We are also familiar with the type of man or woman who is overly dominated by the Eternal Youth. Though more common in the first half of life, there are Puers and Puellas of all ages, and their energy is often a delight during courting. Such a man or woman appears fresh, new, filled with fun, and unpredictable. Life is never dull in the presence of the Eternal Youth in a man or woman. Once this person commits to a relationship, however, then too much of this powerful energy can seem unruly and dangerous. These Puers and Puellas can never commit, fearing that choices may limit their options. They are filled with ideas that are never brought to fruition. Under stress they often become childish, wanting to be babied. In the second half of life, individuals dominated by the Eternal Youth archetype may exhibit immaturity, narcissism, and an inability to grow past the provisional identities established in early adulthood.

Clearly, numerical age is not necessarily equated with maturity.

A widow who came to see me several years ago was stuck trying to decide between two suitors. As she set out to describe the first suitor, she told me that on their first date he had taken her to the park to watch the squirrels play. That was enough for me to picture him, as I immediately could identify the strong presence of the Puer (Eternal Youth). The second suitor was a banker, financially secure and steady as a rock, but a bit stodgy and boring. Which one should she marry?

We talked it back and forth, and then she went away.

A couple of years later I ran into her by chance on the street. We greeted each other, and eventually I asked whom she married.

"Oh, I married Jim, the banker," she said. This was followed by a long silence.

"Well, how is it going?" I asked.

"Oh, fine," she said with an air of resignation, "but he doesn't take me to watch the squirrels play."

In a couple of sentences she had outlined the whole dilemma of the one-sided approach to the two essential archetypal energies. For true maturity, these archetypes must be kept in reasonable balance and dynamic interplay.

A one-sided view of maturity is damaging. What is required for real maturity is not a regression to teenlike irresponsibility or more tiresome responsibility (often interpreted as dutiful obedience to social norms). True maturity involves becoming more response-able, deepening our capacity to respond more flexibly, passionately, and powerfully to life's challenges, to live a life that is self-creating and authentic, and to synthesize the opposites, tempering one with the other.

The Fountain of Youth

The Fountain of Youth is a legendary spring that reputedly restores the youth of anyone who drinks of its waters. Florida is said to be its location, and stories of the fountain are some of the most persistent legends associated with that American state. No wonder so many retirement communities have sprung up there. A long-standing belief is that Spanish explorer Juan Ponce de León was searching for the Fountain of Youth when he traveled to present-day Florida in 1513, but this concept did not start with him; nor was it unique to the New World. Tales of healing waters date back to the ancients. Immortality is a gift frequently sought in mythic stories of treasures, such as the philosopher's stone, universal panaceas, and the elixir of life.

While our modern economy profits from the cult of youth, selling us a plethora of material goods and services with promises of youthfulness, what is really needed as we age is the inner resource of the Eternal Youth. This energy is free, refreshing, and always available. To access it only requires an attitude of tinkering, discovery, and play.

The Spirit of Play

Play may be the simplest thing there is for a child. Children are in a state of perpetual metamorphosis; they have the capacity to move quickly from the fantastic to the everyday and back again, all in a moment. They play *as the spirit moves them*, acting instinctively. As consciousness grows and we experience the complexities of life, however, play becomes a difficult achievement.

When I was a boy, we had a place near the center of town we used to call the "rec," short for recreation center, and it was there that we went to play. In recreation, or re-creation, you have in plain English the association of ideas, which is also found in somewhat abstruse theological writings that emerge from the ancient world. For example, the Sanskrit word *Lila* means "divine play" and refers to the creation, destruction, and re-creation of the universe. The most profound mystery, the unfolding of the cosmos, is understood as divine play, the pleasure of God.

Greeks during the time of Castor and Pollux had a word for play, *paignia*. They personified it as the goddess of playfulness, indicating the importance that it had in their lives. Power, playfulness, and the sacred combined together to make Greek dance, theater, philosophy, and other cultural achievements so timeless and vital.

Gifts of the Monkey God

There is another ancient tale known as the *Ramayana* that I am particularly fond of. This story from India relates one individual's journey through life and his gradual enlightenment. In a notable episode Rama the king is holding court during the morning hours. In those good old days when the king sat on his throne to hold court, anyone in the kingdom could come and lay out their problems and concerns. Justice was to be had at the hands of one's king. The monarch heard the most pressing issues of the day and dispensed justice, wearing his mantle as Wise Elder.

Every morning, as Rama sat on his throne and prepared to hear the long list of petitioners and penitents, a monkey bounced in through the window and brought the king a piece of fruit. This happened daily. Rama became accustomed to this process and didn't pay much attention. He would take the fruit, thank the monkey, toss the fruit behind him, and get on with the business at hand.

Well, a considerable pile of unused and rejected fruit accumulated behind the throne of the wise king. One day they got around to cleaning and discovered a pile of jewels in back of the throne. It seems that every piece of fruit contained a jewel. Hanuman, a manifestation of the divine in the form of a monkey, had presented a gift to the king each morning, and the royal had simply tossed it aside.

Every day of your life Hanuman, the monkey god—your instinctive voice of creative potential—hands you a piece of fruit with a jewel in it. And your inner king, busy with the responsibilities, conflicts, anxieties, and worries of the day, tosses it aside. In back of each person's throne there lies an accumulating heap of gems. These are unlived potentials. They all are available to you, right now, if you open to your archetypal energy.

Symbolic Life Involves Play

In the spirit of play we may toss together elements that were formerly separate, and in this sense symbols are a highly sophisticated form of play. To play is to foster richness of response, to reinterpret reality, to experience life in unforeseen ways. Pure play is different from a game, such as football or a symphony, which has rules and a definite goal. When we watch professional sports on television, we see a highly constricted form of play; even amateur sports increasingly seem to be motivated less by love of the game than by a display of pride or greed, as Stephen Nachmanovitch has pointed out in a marvelous discussion of play and spirituality.[33] The spirit of play can be distorted and destroyed when it is directed to serve the ego's needs. Play is a divine quality that you can bring to anything, an attitude and a presence rather than a defined activity. When play is free, and not choreographed by some existing rules or regulations, it is ambiguous, exciting, risky, and open to possibilities.

To keep the spirit of Eternal Youth active in us during the second half of life, we must learn again to play with our experience. Recall the joy of discovery before it bowed to work, obligation, and duty. Movement is alive; inertia is dead. We become more "unalive" as we cling to that which is predictable and unchanging. Enthusiasm is closely related to the spirit of play—the word comes from the ancient Greek *theos*, meaning "god." To have enthusiasm is to allow yourself to be filled with divine assistance, so the ego does not need to handle your tasks by itself.

Jung kept a notebook filled with writings and sketches. One epigram from Goethe's masterwork *Faust* stands out as a clear inspiration: "Formation, transformation, eternal mind's eternal recreation." While contemplating this epigram, Jung wrote, "The creation of something new is not accomplished by the intellect, but by the play instinct acting from inner necessity. The creative mind plays with the object it loves."[34]

From Childish Games Comes Profound Insight

Active imagination did not come into the world fully formed as a therapeutic technique. In his autobiography, Jung wrote of the period of uncertainty that began for him after a parting of the ways with his professional colleague Freud:

> Above all, I felt it necessary to develop a new attitude toward my patients . . . Thereupon I said to myself, "Since I know nothing at all, I shall simply do whatever occurs to me." Thus I consciously submitted myself to the impulses of the unconscious. The first thing that came to the surface was a childhood memory from perhaps my tenth or eleventh year. At that time I had had a spell of playing passionately with building blocks. I distinctly recalled how I had built little houses and castles. To my astonishment, this memory was accompanied by a good deal of emotion. "Aha," I said to myself, there is still life in these things. The small boy is still around, and possessed a creative life, which I lack. But how can I make my way to it? For as a grown man it seemed impossible to me that I should be able to bridge the distance from the present back to my eleventh year. Yet if I wanted to re-establish contact with that period, I had no choice but to return to it and take up once more his childish games.[35]

Jung noted that it was embarrassing for a professional physician with a long list of patients to be reduced to childish games, but nevertheless, in the time between seeing his patients, he began accumulating stones by the lakeshore and in the sand built small cottages, a castle, and eventually an entire village. He went on with his building game every afternoon for some time. What he found was that in the course of this playful activity his thoughts clarified and he was able to grasp a great stream of fantasies that led to creative breakthroughs. Numerous research papers followed—all growing out of that time playing with stones, sticks, and sand. This experiment later became the basis for numerous therapeutic techniques, including sand tray therapy, dream analysis, and active imagination.

Even the most serious people have play in their daily lives, though they may not think of it that way. A most common form of play is ordinary speech. We draw upon structures provided by our culture, vocabulary and grammar, but the sentences we make up with them are entirely our own. Listen to a conversation in a foreign language, or ignore the content of a conversation in English and notice its process: the cadence, stops and starts, when the voice goes up and down, the rhythm of taking turns. Every conversation can be a playful, creative act.

Writing, painting, surgery, debugging a computer program, invention, "playing" the stock market, tuning an engine, the arts, sports—all creative acts, some of them quite serious—draw upon our capacity to play.

In music, whether singing in the shower, whistling as we rake leaves, or playing an instrument, we are moved by playful impulses. In jazz, or in any improvisational art form, the ideal is a creative moment-to-moment flow, bringing qualities such as luminosity, joy, passion, and depth into the performance. To be vibrantly alive in the moment, we need to be alert to the circumstances presented to us and capable of responding creatively. Of course, you cannot improvise in music without first learning your instrument, and this is true for all endeavors. It will require practice.

In the Christian tradition we are told only those who "become as little children" can enter the kingdom of heaven. In psychological terms this means that we will not experience the numinous and the holy without a childlike, lighthearted quality in our efforts. Notice that I said childlike—not childish. In greater consciousness, the mind is at the utmost point of intensity, involvement, and lucidity.

The Perils of One-sidedness

Running counter to an experimental and dynamic approach to life, the human ego does its best to assimilate reality to existing mental structures. It seeks safety and predictability.

This is rather like the ancient story of Procrustes, another mythic figure from the ancient time of Castor and Pollux. You may have heard of Procrustes' bed. The name *Procrustes* means "he who stretches," and this character is said to have kept a house by the side of the road where he offered hospitality to passing strangers, who were invited in for a pleasant meal and a night's rest in his very special bed. Procrustes described this bed as having the unique property that its length exactly matched whoever lay down upon it. What Procrustes didn't volunteer was the method by which this "one-size-fits-all" was achieved, namely, that as soon as the guest lay down Procrustes went to work upon him, stretching him on the rack if he was too short for the bed and chopping off his legs if he was too tall.

When dominated too much by the Wise Elder archetype, we can become like Procrustes, distorting or cutting off experiences that do not fit our rigid, preconceived ideas.

The Eternal Youth provides a universal solvent for outdated structures. Without this energy we become moribund.

Conversely, more Wise Elder energy is needed when our boundaries are missing or the world seems to be falling apart. I am always amused when someone informs me that they are on the spiritual path and working on getting rid of their ego. If you destroy the ego, you are psychotic, not enlightened. Westerners trying to be rid of the ego often end up with an inflation in the guise of spirit (we are too far gone, too individuated to return to simple pre-egoic consciousness). However, you can move the ego into relationship, in service to something greater. The ego structure can then attend to the practical aspects of keeping a modern life afloat, but it needs to operate on the proper level.

Another way to describe this is to apply the ego as the organ of *awareness* rather than the organ of decision making. This involves a shift of focus from "What's in it for me?" (ego awareness) to "What is needed at this moment for greater wholeness, integration, and creative expression? What serves the greater good?" (higher Self-awareness). I will discuss this evolution of consciousness more extensively in chapter 9.

The Curse of Perfectionism

Perfectionism is a common obstacle to the spirit of the Eternal Youth. An inner critic drives many of us; this is an underdeveloped, destructive form of the Wise Elder that is never satisfied, regardless of our blessings and achievements. Anytime you stiffen or brace yourself against some error or problem, the very act of bracing can cause the problem to occur. This is one reason why children can fall and tumble without getting hurt, while we adults taking the same impact end up at the doctor's office. The road to strength is vulnerability and openness. Mistakes are absolutely essential. Unfortunately, we learn in school that mistakes are something to fear, hide, or avoid.

If you are someone who is cursed by perfectionism, consider how a thermostat operates. A thermostat never has the right temperature. Your house falls a little below the set temperature and the thermostat turns the furnace on. It runs until the house is a little too hot, then it turns the furnace off. It is constantly overshooting the mark, making midcourse corrections, undershooting the mark, adjusting. This is the hallmark of healthy self-organizing systems. The same is true for us—when the ego stays out of the way. Play is the essence of regulating in response to changes in the environment, as psyche must be constantly questioning and answering itself about its own identity.

Watch children at play and you will see great focus and

concentration. There also is a presence, a readiness for whatever happens.

The Zen master Shunryu Suzuki noted that in the beginner's mind there are many possibilities, but in the expert's mind there are few. We are never as pure in our approach as when we first begin something new. The goal of Zen is to maintain this openness and presence at all times. As soon as we begin to discriminate, to rely upon a habitual pattern for sensing reality, we limit ourselves.

Therapy with a Seal

When your work or your life becomes dry, bringing in the playful spirit of the Eternal Youth can lend levity and yeast to your efforts. The healing power of Puer energy can be seen in the midlife turnabout experienced by a man I once knew named Dan.

Dan had been most fortunate in his business dealings so that by the age of thirty he was a millionaire several times over. He was addicted to work, yet despite material success Dan was miserable, perpetually tense, suffering from stomach ulcers, tired of looking after his investments, and locked into an unhappy relationship with his long-time girlfriend. He couldn't afford to leave his business or his relationship—he felt trapped by the very things that defined his life.

Dan and I talked for several sessions about his options, but he didn't seem to make much progress until one day after a session he went for a walk along the beach in Southern California. There is a cove near the world-famous Scripps Aquarium where seals like to gather. It was a weekday afternoon, and Dan found he was the only human sharing the beach that day with a very inquisitive seal. At first they both eyed each other warily, but curiosity eventually got the best of them and the two species decided to approach each other. They hit it off, and before long man and seal were dancing along the beach and then swimming playfully together in the Pacific. Their frolic went on for nearly two hours before they reluctantly agreed to part ways. That experience was transformative.

In our next session Dan could not even get through the door before his story came pouring out. I cheered him on, and by the end of that appointment he announced that he could no longer deny his true nature; he was returning home to do "whatever was necessary." Well, fine, I thought, a seal has been more therapeutic than my best efforts. It had brought Dan's Eternal Youth energy alive again.

A few months later Dan showed up at my door. It had cost him a sizeable sum of money, but he had worked out the details of a separation from his girlfriend, sold his share of the business to a partner, and purchased a thirty-foot sailboat. His session with the seal had pointed the way to a new life. Dan would spend the next several years sailing. He yearned for the freedom and immediacy of the open sea. Over the ensuing years he occasionally took me out to sail with him, and you have never seen anyone more at ease and contented than that man while on the water. The last I heard he had accepted a job with a marine ecology institute. Dan was directly living out his unlived life.

For obvious reasons, not everyone could or would choose to tackle their unlived life as directly as Dan. He was lucky to have the economic resources to make a major life change, and though selling a business he had outgrown and ending an unhappy relationship were painful and expensive, he directly addressed his urgent undeveloped qualities by rearranging things on the outside. If you can do this, fine, but symbolic work through active imagination can be just as effective.

Follow What You Love: An Exercise

Did you know that our tradition of sending notes on Valentine's Day originated with an Italian monk, Valentinus, who in his old age drifted off into an unquenchable love of everyone around him. For enjoyment he began writing notes of appreciation and devotion to more and more people; finally elders at the monastery allowed him to stay in his cell and do nothing but pour out his love by way of his small notes. This was finally honored after his death by beatification.

If you are stuck in the second half of life, weighted down by responsibilities, obligations, and duties (this includes most modern people), then you must find something to love and new ways of bringing joy into your endeavors. What do you have energy and passion for? Write a note to the Eternal Youth who still resides within you. Then place it under your pillow or next to your computer. Your inner being is likely to respond with a dream or a creative outburst. The key is to let go of control or fears of appearing foolish. The unconscious will return to you the attitude that you display toward it. Conduct an active imagination with the images that come to you. What does she or he desire? Follow this energy, and it will get you out of any corner you have painted yourself into.

9

Uniting Life's Oppositions

The oldest ideas we can identify for the Gemini twins seem to come out of India where the two stars were called Aswins, twin horsemen who are harbingers of the dawn. This idea probably goes back some six thousand years to the time when this pair of stars would have appeared just as the sky began to brighten on spring equinox mornings. Thus, the Aswin horsemen were thought of as the forerunners of spring dawn. The concept that these stars symbolized twins apparently spread from India and Persia into Greece, Rome, and then throughout Europe.

Spring dawn. There is something timeless and hopeful about this image of Leda's masculine offspring, Castor and Pollux. They are archetypal symbols of the unity that exists behind every duality.

Zeus's attempt to give Castor and Pollux equal time in Olympus and Hades was a compromise that did not work well in practice. Eventually each of the twins found it too uncomfortable to live in the other's realm. It was only after much suffering that

Zeus found a deeper solution: He divinized Castor, the earthly one, and set both boys into the heavens in eternal embrace. This is a solution not yet widespread in our culture.

To make something conscious that had previously been unconscious is to prepare it to stand in the skies along with its heavenly brother. Then both can take on godly beauty and divinity. Only in this manner can Castor and Pollux embrace on equal levels of nobility. This is a synthesis.

A compromise (letting them spend half their time in Hades and half in Olympus) is a product of the ego and goes no deeper than that. A synthesis is a vision of the original wholeness of the two opposing elements, and this is divine in its origin. Christian theology expresses this by saying that no problem is ever solved on a human level but only by grace. That sounds nice, but it is difficult to truly comprehend.

How do we achieve a true synthesis of the ego and the urgings of the higher Self, of our earthly life and our spiritual calling for wholeness?

Zeus sends Castor into the night sky, making him immortal. Does this mean we should spiritualize our earthy sides? Some might argue that the way out of duality is to "de-earth" our instincts, especially sexuality, disdaining everything earthy about our nature. Some spiritual traditions take this approach. For example, there are advocates of old-time religion who suggest that everything of the body is sinful and is to be at least kept to a minimum. Even fun and joy are suspect. Many of our grandmothers would shake a stern forefinger and admonish, "Now cool that happiness or you will offend our beloved Jesus."

This approach might be excused as a stern measure needed to compensate for the excesses of a materialistic culture, but it is exactly the wrong medicine for our overly abstracted, thought-dominated present age. Perhaps something different is needed as we stand on the edge of a new era. An older old-time religion, our mythic story from Greek civilization, has a different solution.

Try replacing the word *consciousness* with *divinizing*. That which is in the underworld must be made conscious. Does this mean elevating our vices? Wouldn't this threaten the very virtues and values we have worked so hard to elevate in the first half of life?

Every Virtue Has Its Vice

Let's consider a list of "good" values, an unassailable list, as it is drawn from the right-hand side of our personality teeter-totter.

We all know it is good to win; we all prefer to be on the winning side. So much of life is organized to promote winning, and there is no denying that victories are very satisfying. For most people, to win is better than being right.

Anyone can confirm that to receive is also fine. We go to the mailbox in the afternoon to see what has arrived, and when there is a nice check in the mail, or it is payday, or an income tax refund has arrived, this is fine solid stuff and we feel affirmed.

Income is an excellent thing. Nobody doubts it. We ask, "How do you make your living?" and draw conclusions about a person based upon his or her income. Income provides us with a sense of solidity, a measure of our success. It is first-rate to earn. Earning something provides a clean, capable feeling; it is yours—you've earned it. It's fresh.

Similarly, everyone also knows it is good to eat. After a good meal we feel fulfilled. How long till my lunch break? Many of us count the minutes. Meals provide pivot points, adding structure to the day.

Action is excellent. A friend will often advise, "Don't just be passive; go do something. Take control of your life." If you don't like what is going on, it is good to do something about it. If you are lonely, then go meet someone. If you don't have enough money, then get to work. If you don't like your job, get a better one. If you don't support the politicians in office, then organize their replacement. Don't just stand there; do something.

It is also most excellent to own things. Most of us yearn to own a house. Then you are not at the behest of a landlord. It's yours; no one can tell you what to do with your property. You're settled. You're rooted. Similarly, it's great to own an automobile; there is no loan on it—it's yours. Possessions are signs of a good solid sense of self—not only a house and car but all the things we put around us to affirm our being: a computer, a television, a watch, a ring—all of our treasures. Possessions are extensions of who we are; they provide handles so that others can get hold of us. They are signs of a healthy sense of accomplishment, of a successful life.

It's also considered a good quality to stay busy; busy hands are happy hands. The devil is the result of idle hands. When we get up in the morning, how fine it is to have a cup of coffee and plan our day. As my father used to say, "Let's get out there and do something, even if it's wrong."

Sex is certainly fine; it is related, it's touching, it's folding oneself back into the body of nature, it is transcending oneself, the ultimate form of giving. Eros makes the world go round.

Being decisive is also a virtue. Don't be a mealy-mouthed person who can't say where you stand on an issue. It's great to be in the presence of people who are decisive; you know what to expect from them. To be elected to office requires decisiveness; if you change your mind or reconsider a position based on new information, you will be labeled a flip-flopper.

Freedom is certainly good; the U.S. Constitution and the American way of life are built on freedom to choose. Choice is an excellent thing, a hallmark of consciousness and a high virtue.

Democracy is very good; we fight and die for it. We wage wars around the world to keep it safe. Power also is good, as long as it is in the right hands. Those with personal power are the ones who get elected, or who stand at the pulpit on Sunday, or who get the promotions. The head of the bank, the lawyer, the doctor— these are professions that wield power and so they are usually well rewarded.

Sobriety most certainly is a high virtue; we ask of those who hold power to also be capable of sobriety.

Clarity is first-class; it is nice to be around people who are clear. People said that Winston Churchill was a great man because he was always unambiguous. If you asked his opinion on an issue, he would tell you point-blank, "This is where I stand." If it turned out to be wrong, Churchill generally would admit it. When you are confused or lost, it is a relief to get a clear answer or clear directions.

Consciousness is also a high virtue, certainly among those who are interested in psychology, spirituality, self-improvement, and personal growth. To be conscious is to be aware, to be awake, to be alert—these are superior indeed.

I will stop here with this excellent list of virtues, though the enumeration could go on and on. You could assemble your own list of values that you believe to be right and true. Surely no one would argue with advocacy for such fine qualities, and most of us have spent at least half a lifetime pursuing them.

What About the Opposite?

Now let's stand these noble ideals on their heads. What is the spiritual point of view regarding these virtues?

Wisdom traditions from across all times and cultures have insisted that it is better to lose than to win, better to give than to receive. We were all told this as children—was it just childish prattle to keep us in line? The Bible pointedly states: Sell all that you have and give to the poor; the rich man has as much chance of reaching heaven as a camel passing through the eye of a needle. As for earning, the spiritual seeker learns that possessions just get in the way. Early Christianity had nothing to do with ownership, which was considered anathema to a life devoted to God.

Traditional wisdom also suggests that it is better to fast than to eat; a man who fasts for forty days and forty nights in the desert is preparing himself to encounter the divine. Fasting honors holy days.

As for action, we are earnestly informed that it is better to turn the other cheek.

With respect to busyness, saints are renowned for long periods of silence and inaction; and when it comes to sexuality, celibacy and chastity are extolled as virtues—you save energy for God rather than give it indiscriminately to the world.

Decisiveness? A spiritual seeker is advised to listen to the will of God, not to vainly pursue his or her own desires. A monk or nun takes a vow of obedience and gives up his or her freedom. Buddhists believe you are only free when there is no choice left, as freedom produces anxiety, and suffering arises from pre-ference. Every choice produces one-sidedness that corrodes our contentment.

Democracy is not the way of the spiritual order; you follow the word and deed of the preacher, the master, the yogi, the shaman, the rabbi, the law, and the pope. As for power, everyone knows that power corrupts and absolute power corrupts absolutely. Power is the opposite of love—seeking power is the desire to control the other, while love is the desire to be one with the other. Where there is unconditional love there is no issue of power. From the religious point of view, love is much preferred. "Love knows all things, love conquers all things, and love endures all things."

What about consciousness? From the religious perspective the meditative state, the inner world, is much superior to outer reality. In the East, the stuff of consciousness is called *maya*, a word that translates as "illusion." When you think that you are conscious and focused and reasonable, you are actually only indulging in maya. Additionally, you won't find God if you are too precisely focused on *your* agenda (although focus is excellent for getting to work on time, finishing your income tax forms, or building a car). The true seeker desires expanded awareness.

While our culture may privilege sobriety, the devotee of God hungers for ecstasy. Abandoning yourself to the winds of God— there is nothing sober about that.

So here we have two sets of values and virtues. On the right-hand side are some of the primary qualities we hold dear and celebrate in our culture, but the second list seems to contradict them at every step. In fact, there is no list of virtues that cannot be contradicted. Here is another example: We are told that humility is a high virtue, but if a person has debilitating low self-esteem, what is needed at that time is more, not less, pride. We can also see that anger, one of the so-called cardinal sins, is an appropriate response in the face of oppression.

Is this the dreaded moral relativism warned about every Sunday by television evangelists? Or is it just the nature of reality?

Jung predicted that we are ushering in a new era that requires a new ethic, and wrote that we might define this new ethic as "a development and differentiation within the old ethic, confined at present to those uncommon individuals who, driven by unavoidable conflicts of duty, endeavor to bring the conscious and the unconscious into responsible relationship."[36]

The old ethic was based upon a set of absolute values and principles that were to be followed to achieve moral perfection while maintaining social order and well-being. It maintains that good and evil are contradictory opposites so that certain thoughts, feelings, and behaviors must be avoided or we find ourselves in a position of sin. This ethic fails to advance the impetus of the second half of life, the development of greater authenticity, wholeness, and unity,[37] and it is the product of a consciousness that we must grow past if our planet is to survive.

There are two kinds of oppositions: contradictory opposites, which cancel each other out (such as right/left or up/down), and contrary opposites, which blend together and are never really separated (such as light/dark or health/sickness). For example, as I write these words, the sky outside my window has shifted from dark to partial light as the sun rises, to more light, and then to more darkness as a cloud passes by. Similarly, we never are completely healthy but always experience a dynamic process of health and sickness. The dualistic viewpoint of the old ethic encourages a splitting rather than a union because it maintains that good and evil are contradictory opposites. Innate and natural thoughts and emotions are unlived. Repressed, they fall into the unconscious, where they eventually come back to haunt us as neurotic symptoms or projections upon others whom we distrust and resist. It has been wisely noted that bad moods are often the result of chronic virtuousness.

In black and white thinking (contradictory opposites), we must choose either/or. It is tempting to engage in this type of thinking when we are confronted with paradox, but paradox is an artesian well of meaning that we need so badly in our modern world. Contradiction is static, while paradox makes room for grace and mystery. What appears to be contradiction at one level of consciousness becomes paradox when perceived from a broadened perspective. Yet we must continue to live and act in the earthly realm. What are we to do with this?

To Act Is to Sin

If you take the paradoxical aspect of life wrongly, then you are condemned to suffer and will probably end up cynical and disillusioned. You cannot act and yet you cannot *not* act. Even when you choose one side for a time, the presence of the contradictory value eventually spoils it. If we attempt to live an examined life, like St. Augustine or any of the other saints, we soon find that, as Augustine wrote, "to act is to sin." The reclamation of unlived life is a profoundly deep immersion in paradox, which is one reason we don't do very well with it at first.

We refuse the paradoxical nature of reality, translating it into opposition. For example, when play is torn loose from work, both are spoiled. Personal suffering results whenever we are caught between two apparent oppositions.

A prevailing attitude in our culture is that the "other" is to be projected away or pushed down as completely as possible, so that instead of reclaiming unlived life as our divine right and an act of profound meaning, we instead see it only in others and bury it deep within ourselves. So often we are repulsed by the opposite of the ego's current list of "truth" that we project the opposite qualities elsewhere—on a sibling, a coworker, people from another ethnic or religious group, a foreign culture. This is the old, primitive, scapegoat method of placing qualities perceived as negative on another person or tribe, and then hating them for what we don't want to deal with in ourselves. This tribal mentality has become increasingly dangerous in our interdependent and interconnected world. If we persist in this old method of dealing with what is incomplete and unfinished in us, it will blow us up. Fanaticism is always a sign that one has adopted one side of a pair of opposites. Half of the truth must be kept at bay since this kind of righteousness depends on "being right."

When you refuse ownership of your own missing pieces, you inevitably damage someone. This is a terrible thing to do—true sin.

Everything that conscious human beings experience is brought to us in pairs of opposites. Anything you do or can experience in your life always has some unlived opposite in the unconscious. Truths always come in pairs, and we endure this so we can be in accord with reality. Most of the time we support two warring points of view and evade the confrontation. For example, I need to go to work, but I don't want to; I don't like my neighbor, but I still must be civil with him or her; I should lose some weight, but I like certain foods so much. We live with contradictions like these on a daily basis.

You cannot just eliminate one side of the balance, and it is not healthy to cast the "vices" upon your neighbor. But you can change your way of looking at the problem. The two sides need not be viewed as contradictory. Good and evil are not contradictory opposites. They exist in contrary relationship to each other; that is, they increase and decrease in relationship to each other, and both are necessary. When you embrace both sides of the opposing elements in full consciousness, you embrace paradox. True religious experience occurs exactly at the point of insolubility.

Try to allow both sides of any issue to exist in equal dignity and worth. If you sit with the tension, a solution that is better than either one will emerge. The two forces will teach each other something and produce new insight.

To advance from opposition (always a quarrel) to paradox (always holy) is to make a leap of consciousness. Paradox forces us beyond ourselves and destroys naïve and inadequate adaptations and compromises.

As already noted, the Hindu word *maya* means "illusory." Maya is the trickery or game we all get caught up in, trying to get through the daily entanglements of life. Sometimes maya is translated into English as "that which is not true." However, there is an extension of this concept, and it is known as *maha maya*, the word *maha* meaning "great." *Maha maya*, the "great illusion" is a divine game. Who is right and who is wrong? Which virtue is more important to actualize? Which side of reality takes precedence? *Maha maya* is the great game that we all are playing. Whether your life is going right or wrong (and on the human, cultural level we all are concerned with trying to decipher and navigate our way through this world of opposition and struggle), each personal experience also is a slice of the greater drama.

What About Evil?

A theologian was once paraphrasing Thomas Aquinas, saying that evil is the absence of good. "Don't forget the rest of the sentence," said a wise old monk. No one knew there was more to the sentence. The missing part of the sentence is "that ought to be there." So, the correct reading is: "Evil is the absence of good *that ought to be there.*" What does this mean?

Slowly I have begun to understand what Thomas Aquinas and the old monk were getting at. If you substitute the word *consciousness* for the word *good*, this statement becomes very useful. Then this church father would be saying, "Evil is the absence of consciousness that ought to be there." In other words, a new sum of energy that is unlived but has matured enough in the underworld to make its way to consciousness cannot be ignored. The absence of something ready for consciousness that is denied or repressed is a cause of evil.

This idea provides a gauge for which aspects of our shadows we should pay attention to—those that are urgent and available to consciousness. (This also addresses the notion that missionary work should be to go out and enlighten the heathens of the world with the "Truth," be it the Christian truth, the Muslim truth, the scientific truth, the therapeutic truth, or any other particular slice of reality. If people are not ready for it, particularly in the dogmatic form that missionaries often are trying to sell, there is no use pestering them.) Unless a bit of reality presents itself to us in an urgent form from our own psyche, it is not going to take. It must be available to our consciousness, not a transplant that someone else thinks is important.

Every possibility in us is worthy of and deserves consciousness but not necessarily expression. Those aspects of unlived life that are ready to be made conscious but are refused are the ones that cause the trouble. Symptoms, accidents, dreams—these all are ways that the higher Self tells us if something critical to our fulfillment has been refused. You may start to get headaches or a sore back, or perhaps you are tired all the time. Or maybe you have a disturbing and repetitive dream. For you to find what is wrong, it is the unconscious not the conscious ego that must do the sorting. It is remarkable that there *is* something in the unconscious that is capable of sorting. If you listen to your symptoms, they will produce an image that can be utilized in conscious life to initiate change.

It follows that something repressed is in the wrong place; it is not inherently good or bad, just misplaced. From a God's-eye view, there is nothing that does not belong in the psyche—there are only things that have been applied incorrectly. Our error consists of misplacing or misapplying some potential at the wrong time and then calling it bad.

Evolution from Either/Or to Both/And

Everything the human mind can comprehend appears to be made up of pairs of opposites. We are generally incapable of seeing beyond that. Jung once said the medieval mentality is either/or, but if humanity is to survive, we must learn to cope with both/and. Another Greek myth addresses one aspect of our divided state: it tells that humans originally had four legs and four arms and carried both male and female characteristics. At some point we were split, and the two parts have been trying to get back together ever since.

In an unexpected way necessity protects us from taking the contradictions of life head-on. But as our standard of living gets better and we have more leisure time, the tension of the opposites only increases. When life is hard, necessity settles many things. This is perhaps why most people can't stand too much freedom—this idea isn't very popular and may be heard as downright un-American, but the more freedom, the more anxiety arises as a result of the ego-based level of awareness. This is the experience of duality.

Achievement of a more penetrating consciousness to unite life's oppositions is the lifting of that veil. If you try to think about a unitive vision beyond duality, you have already fractured it into the human dimension. But we do get glimpses of what it would be like to live out of a place of unity and wholeness. Krishnamurti once said that the chief obstacle to heaven is our ideas about heaven, and I believe this to be true.

To get on the path to enlightenment, instead of approaching life as a series of contradictions that must be fought, you can fatefully embrace what happens in daily life. This implies taking the ego and investing it somewhere. If your power and freedom are invested fatefully, you will be saved from the constant anxiety of a split world. To remove this anxiety you need only say yes to *what is*. So simple, but not easily accomplished.

Building God's Cathedral

There's a wonderful story set in medieval times in which a man sees a laborer walking by with a wheelbarrow and asks what he is doing. "Can't you see, I'm pushing a wheelbarrow," the laborer replies. Another man comes by doing the same thing and he, too, is asked, "What are you doing?" He replies, "Can't you see, I'm performing the work of God; I'm building Chartres Cathedral."

The same activity, but very different levels of awareness. The second man has invested his work fatefully—connected to a greater purpose—and thereby rendered his life meaningful. It's not what you do in life that is most important; rather, it's a question of what consciousness you bring to the activity. Whether you are pushing a wheelbarrow or heading a corporation is really not the point. Who is doing it and what consciousness is brought forth?

If we can accept that ego consciousness is implicitly a dual consciousness—endlessly splitting reality up into this and that, what is chosen and what is unchosen, what is lived and what is unlived—then we are ready to advance beyond duality.

When India was about to tear itself to pieces right after its liberation from Great Britain, there were riots everywhere. New Delhi was already burning, and Calcutta was the worst hotbed of chaos and violence. Hindus were setting fire to Muslim homes, and vice versa. Mohandas Gandhi responded by getting on a train to Calcutta; after arriving he went to the home of a Muslim friend, set up his string bed overlooking the main thoroughfare, and announced that he was going to fast unto death. The news that Gandhi was there traveled like wildfire through the neighborhoods, and gradually the situation was calmed. That's the reconciling power of a symbol. Gandhi was a walking symbol of reconciliation. We generally think of people like that as sages or saints. Yet powerful symbols of such magnitude show up in the psyches of each of us.

Wouldn't it be great to just let go of your ego? Just live in the now and be enlightened?

Buddhist teachers say that anything you do to escape fundamental duality just kicks more energy into it. Your only choice is to stop. That unsplit, unifying place—beyond ordinary human ego awareness—is found at the fulcrum. This is the holy place, the whole place. The demand for human consciousness to have the "right" thing at the exclusion of something else just sets the wheel in motion again.

Saying Yes to What Is

It might appear that the best solution is to do nothing, but that is not exactly right. There is a kind of consciousness that assists slowing down. This idea was introduced in chapter 4 in the discussion of being as opposed to doing. From the place of being we can observe what is and accept it through what I call creative suffering. This is not passively accepting a miserable life or stoically gritting your teeth or cynically expecting the worst. That is neurotic suffering. Creative suffering is both accepting and active. The word *suffer* in its original sense means "to allow," such as in one of Shakespeare's dramas when a courtier says, "I suffer you to speak before the king." So to suffer creatively is simply to allow what is, to stop fighting it, and instead to affirm your life.

Creative suffering is allowing *what is* and saying "yes!" Such experience is redemptive in that it leads to healing and self-knowledge. If you can honestly assess what is true in your life, looking at it with objectivity and intelligence, you are getting closer to enlightenment, as your escape mechanism is diminished. By stating *what is* at any moment, with complete honesty and sincerity, you become conscious of it.

When God "divided the light from the darkness," as we are told in Genesis, it was not that the darkness was left over as something that was not of God, but that both the light and the darkness were in God. The same goes for every pair of opposites that you can conceive: hot and cold, rough and smooth, wet and dry, pleasure and pain. It is one of the principal rules of the game that opposites come in pairs.

This notion is encountered in the writings of a huge number of mystics the world over, during all ages, and from within all faith traditions. William Blake expressed it succinctly when he wrote in "Auguries of Innocence":

> *Joy and woe are woven fine,*
> *A clothing for the soul divine;*
> *Under every grief and pine*
> *Runs a joy with silken twine.*
> *It is right it should be so;*
> *Man was made for joy and woe;*
> *Through the world we safely go.*[38]

Blake is pointing out the discovery of how opposites may be brought into harmony. When this is accomplished, "Through the world we safely go."

Contemplating this, we can speculate about the origin of the Christian doctrine of original sin. To be human is to be based in sin (which we can take to be the tension between opposites—not as inherently bad). To escape from this costs us the loss of the human condition—a crucifixion of our usual ego consciousness. Taking this a step further, is our human condition set in opposition to another, deeper consciousness? At any given moment can we experience the split world or the heavenly realm but not both?

It is a fact of life that, like Castor and Pollux, we all experience a fall from wholeness into divided, differentiated consciousness. And it also is a fact of the human condition that something in us never stops seeking unification. It is extremely difficult for the human mind to comprehend a unified realm without tearing it into pieces, which distorts it. Still, we have to cope with it somehow.

I have proposed that, viewed from a certain level of awareness, reality is singular, not split into oppositions, but when we attempt to work out a technique for achieving such consciousness we invariably are left choosing between possibilities. This is an untenable contradiction.

If you watch your own process carefully, you will discover that there is a level in back of the split, which was of a different character than the consciousness seeing the split. We must then ask: Do we project the appearance of duality from our own consciousness onto a nonsplit world? Does this imply that we can find a nonsplit consciousness if we learn how to quiet our egos?

Our search is for that consciousness that is not divided in the first place. The solution to the problem is not to solve it but to *dissolve* the split. This brings us to what Jung called the *psychoid* realm, which obeys different laws from our everyday dualistic world. The ego cannot set up what is "real," because its own polarity determines the relativity of its statements. Jung believed that psychic events are founded upon a psychoid base, which is commonly referred to as spiritual. In that realm, human consciousness (the ability to discern) and objective reality (unsplit) merge. There is no collision between them. Is this a convoluted way of discovering the original meaning of prayer? If so, that noble word has strayed far from its original meaning.

Practically speaking, if we spend as much time being alert and aware as we do worrying, we would be out of any mess fairly soon. Often when a client comes to the consulting room burdened down just past endurance, at the breaking point, I tell the client, "In this hour I can take half of the burden off you, and the rest you will have to bear." That seems like a good bargain to most people. The half that I take off is the rebellion against the process, the situation as it is. If you stop struggling with it, half of the burden is removed. Then you have to work to deal with the half that remains. When you stop fighting your situation, you still have the situation but you no longer have the struggle to cope with. Generally we can endure that. This is to cease wounding yourself on the jailhouse bars of reality—to stop complaining about what is.

Dissolving the Split Perspective: An Exercise

Choose a polarity in your life that you want to explore, such as work and play, love and power, dutifulness and spontaneity. Take a sheet of paper and on one side create a drawing that represents one of the poles you have chosen. Then turn the sheet over and make a drawing on the opposite side representing the other pole. Don't worry about the artistic quality of your drawings; just let your hand move freely. If you are overly self-conscious, try drawing with your nondominant hand.

Now notice how the two poles of this opposition in your life are facing each other. Imagine an interaction going on between them. Then take a clean sheet of paper and draw an interaction of the figures or images. Allow them to intermix. This may take the form of a clash, a tentative dialogue, or distant communication. Continue drawing on new sheets of paper, allowing this dialogue of opposites to evolve. The elements in your drawings may begin to change spontaneously.

When a synthesis appears in a new drawing, ask yourself what it represents, and be aware of the inner state that produced the image. Then reflect on how this new synthesis could manifest in your life.

10

Returning Home and
Knowing It for the First Time

On their way back home from helping Jason to recover the Golden Fleece, Castor and Pollux were sailing on a stormy ocean. It was then that a violent and deadly hurricane struck their ship. Everyone on board expected that the wine dark sea would soon be his grave. Orpheus played upon his harp while everyone prayed, and when the storm suddenly abated, it is said that stars appeared upon the heads of Castor and Pollux, as though they had been sanctified.

From this miracle, Castor and Pollux afterward came to be considered guardians of voyagers. The gods blessed them, perhaps an intimation of their later deification in the night sky. Sailors in the ancient world invoked the names of Castor and Pollux whenever they witnessed the shimmering, radiant light, which in certain states of the atmosphere appear around ship sails in the form of fire at the masthead (this phenomenon is also known as St. Elmo's fire). A jet of this mysterious light during a storm is considered a good omen, for it tends to occur in the dissipating stages when the most violent surface winds and seas are abating. Its appearance portends that the spirits of Castor and Pollux are present as guides.

In their youth, Castor and Pollux were heroic. In their later years, they incorporated a godlike nature as a synthesis of both personalities. Statues and temples were erected to the Gemini twins, and their images were carved as figureheads on ships. Indeed, the Apostle Paul sailed on such a ship from the Isle of Melita on his journey to Rome. In Acts 28:11 we read: "And after three months we departed in a ship of Alexandria which had wintered in the isle, whose sign was Castor and Pollux."

Images representing the duo also were placed on Roman coins and Babylonian boundary stones as well as on charts of the sky. Most recently, they have been honored again in human history as a critical part of our journey into space: Project Gemini placed two men aboard a spacecraft into earth orbit. Like Argonauts of old, American astronauts went in quest of experience and greater awareness of our place in the cosmos.

Re-Centering the Universe

We, too, can incorporate divine vision into our earthly existence. But to accomplish this requires a re-centering. A little more than five hundred years ago, the astronomer Nicolaus Copernicus challenged the notion that the earth is the center of the physical universe. He and Galileo Galilei, an Italian scientist who formulated the basic law of falling bodies, verified a new cosmology. Galileo constructed a telescope with which he studied lunar craters, and through careful observation he espoused the Copernican cause. Psychologically speaking, it is a similar heresy today to suggest that the ego is not the center of individual reality. Contemporary society goes to ridiculous lengths to keep up this illusion. In our mature years, however, this paradigm begins to reach the limits of credibility.

The Western world invented the concept of a personal "I," and Western languages are, for the most part, egocentric in structure. We have inherited religious traditions that speak at another level, but they have become ineffective because religious institutions fall victim to the paradox of identity, focusing more on structures, rules, and regulations than on re-centering our lives around an enduring locus and helping us to navigate numinous experiences.

For a contemporary person, God is somebody—often a father—and prayer is the attempt to get our way with him. An unspoken aim of science is to make things go the way we want them to go—to change this, create that, negate something else. The collective trend is to worship science and technology and follow an ethos that consists almost entirely of telling God what to do—in polite language, of course. But this is a constricted frame of reference. Secular and sacred institutions alike have become egoic structures. We arrogantly strive to remake nature and God in our own image.

There Is Only the Dance

In his *Four Quartets*, T. S. Eliot wrote:

> *At the still point of the turning world. Neither flesh nor fleshless;*
> *Neither from nor towards;*
> *At the still point, there the dance is,*
> *But neither arrest nor movement. And do not call it fixity,*
> *Where past and future are gathered.*
> *Neither movement from nor towards,*
> *Neither ascent nor decline. Except for the point, the still point,*
> *There would be no dance, and there is only the dance.*[39]

Eliot perceived the dance of creation, a dance that physicists now find in the ordered play of subatomic particles (the final unity of matter and spirit). Eliot's vision, which became ripe in his old age, is of a meeting of time and space, where one must let go of all the thoughts and theories that have defined one in the past. He asks for forgiveness of his good as well as his bad actions in life. It is a new language he seeks that is beyond definition in words, beyond opposites, a language heard for centuries by the mystics, sages, and great artists. In so-called primitive societies it was expressed unconsciously in the nature of their dances.

Memories become more vivid and meaningful as we look back over the stories of our lives. If a life review is done with candor and honesty, we will see just how many of our acts and achievements, which at the time seemed virtuous and good, were also inadvertently the cause of harm. How much damage and pain is inflicted in the name of the good and the true?

There is only one answer to the contradictions of this world of cause and effect: those of us willing to integrate the opposites within ourselves may enter into the dance of all creation. The poet's imagery of the dance and of coming home to know it for the first time is potent. I return to the verse from Eliot that prefaced this book:

We shall not cease from exploration
And the end of all our exploring
Will be to arrive where we started
And know the place for the first time.

Circumambulating the still point at the center, we see that life moves in spirals. It is no longer a straight line from birth to death, but instead we may come to perceive life as a series of patterns or dances within the dark of creation. We may approach what Jung called the central secret of life. Having distinguished the ego from the greater circumference of the higher Self, we consciously enter the dance.

Achieving Our Death

Jung suggested that each of us must achieve our death.

A life directed to a goal and purpose is far healthier and

richer than an aimless life, and death is the natural goal of every existence. Shrinking away from this goal robs the second half of life of its purpose. A dying person who cannot let go of life is as neurotic and stuck as a young person who is unable to embrace it. In many cases, the same childish greediness, fears, defiance, and willfulness are displayed in both situations. This is why all religions, which view death as only a transition, are psychologically as well as spiritually health-promoting. Since time began people have felt the need to believe in a continuance of life, and the images that arise in dreams and symbolic work show no signs of the psyche ending with physical death.

Just as colleges introduce our young people to knowledge of the world important for the first half of life, there should be colleges for forty-, fifty-, and sixty-year-olds to prepare them for the challenges of the second half, such as old age, death, and eternity.

It is told that when Saint Francis was dying, with his brother monks around him, he asked that his clothes be taken off so he could meet his maker without any barrier. The monks agreed to this. Later he asked, "Please put me on the floor, as I want to be nearer my mother." His last words were "Lord, you made me this way, so please take me this way." I have taken comfort from that story.

After a certain number of years each of us will die. This is inevitable. If we just think of death as the end of our life, we have an inadequate understanding. On the other hand, if we think that we do not die, this also is wrong. We die, and we do not die. In Western societies we harbor the notion that "I" is a unique individual, and enlightenment must consist of bringing one's uniqueness to an absolute pitch. An Easterner would call enlightenment the extinguishment of one's individuality. If you ask a guru in India about continuing to exist after death, he or she is likely to respond: Does the dewdrop still exist after it falls back into the ocean? While you puzzle that out rationally, the guru has gone on to afternoon tea. Of course the dewdrop still exists, though no longer as a dewdrop. The extinction of the personality is tempered by the idea that the truly enlightened person is also a compassionate person, which means he or she is aware of the rest of humankind and expends energy teaching and assisting others.

Most of us shiver with repulsion at the prospect of death, forgetting that whenever one sort of experience is upon us, its opposite must always be close by. Death is closely associated with ecstatic experience. The word *ecstasy* comes from the Greek and means "to stand outside oneself." The ego becomes fearful of such experiences and thinks, "God save me from that!" The ecstatic experience is never conscious; it occurs outside of consciousness. When ecstatic possibilities arise, the ego attempts to extinguish them as quickly as possible. When we are in great suffering, we can be sure that God is too close for comfort.

The more wisdom sets in, the greater the realization that, in the end, we know very little about who we truly are. Jung wrote: "The older I have become, the less I have understood or had insight into myself." Instead of defining ourselves by what we are not, we feel our oneness with all. We begin to sense our connection with all people and things, to glimpse the meaning of "I am" as the name of God. This achievement is not an enantiadromia, the turning of the opposites experienced at midlife. Rather, it is the dawning of awareness of the unity of seemingly opposed attitudes toward life. We begin to grasp a new vision, to see the dance of God in everything. This dance is uniquely expressed in you, in me, and in every detail of the incarnate world. This is to become sanctified and unified.

Throughout this book, on every issue, I have attempted to point out how human consciousness becomes stuck with the unrealized opposite of every choice that is made. Stamping out the unlived portion of life doesn't work; that is the pre-Copernican heresy (be good, choose the "right" things, and you will go to heaven). But then the "wrong" thing becomes unconscious and unlived, and it comes back to terrorize us. In our drive to dominate and control, what comes back to our society as the rejected and unlived? To take but one example, our greatest invention— atomic energy—turns into our greatest danger. The irony we are facing today is that terrorists or a firebrand state may obtain atomic power and use it to destroy us.

At this crucial turning point in history we must learn to live the unlived life. We must find a conscious place for what is underdeveloped, repudiated, and cast off. The unlived quantity must be brought into the whole because it turns out that our egocentric position is not the center of the universe after all and that there is something to be learned from what is missing.

The pre-Copernican man says, "Look, it's perfectly obvious, the sun rises in the morning. Are you an idiot? Anyone can see that. The earth is the center of the universe." But Copernicus saw differently. What is real? If you look up the origin of the word *real*, you will find that it is derived from "royal"; in other words, it is whatever the king (or the authority in power) says. We might wish reality was that simple, but those days are gone.

We understand today from quantum physics that what is "real" is relative and always involves the interaction with the observer making the observation. Still, the everyday, practical world clings to the prejudices of the old paradigm and persists in thinking that what is real is what we perceive consciously with our puny tools of perception. It's true, we have to maintain and honor a fragment of reality, the egocentric attitude, but what about those fragments that don't get included, those aspects that don't fit the established paradigm? We cannot disregard the effects of gravity or the local laws by which we live (such as driving on the designated proper side of the road), but we must acknowledge that they are local, and not enough to account for the whole. This requires humility and surrender of certainty.

What to Do with the Mess?

I must state again: Nothing exists in our human dimension without its opposite close by.

I once designed and built a special clavichord, a very exotic instrument called a Clavichord d'Amour. None have survived from the seventeenth or eighteenth centuries when this beautiful instrument held a high place in the musical world; only one paragraph could be found in an obscure treatise describing its physical structure, followed by long paragraphs extolling the fineness of its tone.

After I spent two winters of spare time in the designing and building, a fine instrument resulted. While working on this project, I was daily reminded of the polarity of all experience: shuffling around in piles of wood shavings, companioned by glue pots and a general mess of cast-off wood and metal. The glue was the old horsehide concoction, perfect for inlay work. How to make horsehide glue? You skin an old horse, boil its hide for a week, skim the fat off, boil it down to the proper consistency, and what are you left with? Mess. That is the lesson I learned on the search to find the dulcet tones of the Clavichord d'Amour—possibly the most delicate and refined sound ever known to humankind.

What about the mess that we all make daily with any activity we undertake? And what about the poor horse? Mess! How do we cope with this inevitable reality in our pursuit of the beautiful and the true?

There is no way around it but to plunge into this collectively proscribed subject. At risk of rudeness, it must be said that our shadows and our shit have remarkable parallels. To create or choose the good is to extract what we value from the vast array of stuff that greets us from all sides; the alchemists called this stuff the *prima materia*, the material from which all creation springs. We eat natural food, extract from it what is useful to us, and excrete the rest.

Humankind seems to be the single—or at least the principal— carrier of the search for the good. The rest of creation seems content to take what is, or at least to follow its instinctive patterns of the right way to do things. Humans, on the contrary, are not easily content and want to improve everything we touch. To return to our example, improving the state of wood and glue, the metal and varnish, to make something better of it, the end result was quite wonderful—a clavichord that produces beautiful music, but we are in severe danger if we lose track of the mess made in the process. The same is true for the world in which we find ourselves today. We seem to be up to our elbows in messes.

The Christian era, which held sway in the West for centuries, drifted off into a sleight of hand, convincing itself that there is no mess or at least that it is polite to hide it and pretend that it does not exist. So much of our day-to-day cultural world consists of playing as if we don't have perspiration or dandruff or smell like a goat after exercising or make frequent trips to the toilet. Carried to its extreme, we cannot even tolerate direct names for the toilet we use daily. The word *toilet* turned into *lavatory*, which turned into *bathroom*, which turned into *restroom*, which turned into *washroom*, which turned into *WC*, which turned into. . . . The reluctance to face our own shit is very strong.

Hesitation to give dignity to our sexual nature is far worse than our unease in the lavatory department. Christianity departed from its most basic tenet—that Christ (the prototype of man) is equal parts Man and God, equal parts Earth and Heaven. Much of basic theology concerns itself with this fact and the word *heresy* originally meant "to be off balance"—to overrate one side or the other of this basic equilibrium. To degrade the human, earthy side of humanity is to break the central teaching of Christianity. Yet the attitude in many churches today is that the body is to be denied, mortified, given the smallest possible place in human functioning.

What happened?

One possibility is that ancient peoples, and continuing on into the Middle Ages, were so immersed in the physical world that they desperately needed to be moved from this one-sided position to the desired paradox of man/god, earth/heaven—which is the deepest teaching of Christianity. A great structure of ceremonies and disciplines was built up around the medieval person to draw him or her away from the heretical position of too much earth and not enough spirit. Old societies protected people from direct contact with the divine, perhaps understanding that only a few people could withstand the impact of a vision of God. Much of traditional religious ceremony consisted of protecting people from numinous experience that might be too much for them. The shaman or priest provided an intermediary between the two worlds. This served well and spoke directly to the needs of people in earlier times. But modern people overshot the process and relegated earth, body, and sex to an inferior position. We are in need of balancing as badly as medieval man was, but our need is quite the opposite. Today, sexuality and romantic love attempt to carry the burden of our lost connection with the numinous—but without the necessary link to the transcendent.

Many of our religious disciplines—both West and East—are designed for an imbalance that is 180 degrees different from our present needs. In fact, it is impossible to say what each person needs now in any collective sense; one individual may still need to be drawn out of a mortal Castor clumsiness, while another person may need to have his or her earthy sense rescued from the overidealistic, theoretical Pollux mentality that threatens to tear life completely out of its human rootedness. Now the import of our guiding story becomes more apparent: We must learn to synthesize the mortal (Castor) and the immortal (Pollux) sides of our nature into a new unity. But how?

No Simple Recipes

Never was the old proverb "One man's meat is another man's poison" more applicable. If someone is drowning, don't try to resuscitate him by throwing a pail of water in his face; or another man may be dying for lack of the same water and does not need more discipline and abstractions but a dousing of water.

Unfortunately, there is no simple recipe for finding your unity and fulfillment. Obviously, the first thing is to become aware of your own heresy. Is your life too flooded or too dry? Are you refined to the point of enervation and in need of some of the unlived material that has been rejected as useless? Is your earthy connection so strong as to exclude your visionary Pollux nature? Just this insight is halfway to the restoration of wholeness (holiness).

In becoming whole, you must start where you are, even if waking up only half an hour before your death. You don't have to power your way through every step. All that is required is to make the unconscious conscious. You must learn to live *your* unlived life. Speaking it aloud to another human being—the ancient practice of confession—is enough to redeem a sin. Of course, it is morally good and right to repair what you can in outer life, but psychically, the only requirement is that you become aware, put the opposites back together. As noted earlier, I am not referring to an indiscriminate wholeness but rather your particular relationship to everything else. You become more whole by working through the specificity of your life, not by trying to evade or rise above the particulars of your life. What is really true about your current situation?

A true confession is a small crucifixion, a facing of a pair of opposites that have been torn apart. You can't "do" anything until the synthesis of consciousness takes place. Trying to clean up some mess you've made before this synthesis almost always just makes more mess. Most doing is just wriggling in the flypaper.

Another word must be updated if we are to avoid a stalemate; *heavenly* must be enlarged to include earth. Heaven is not some other time or some other place but is here and now; and it is here and now that the process of the divinization of Castor must be accomplished.

The Twilight Years

We speak of the challenges of midlife, but could there be another dramatic shift that occurs in the twilight of life? We say that someone is growing old, referring alike to those who are being dragged into the last stage of existence and those who are still actually learning and developing wisdom.

As we enter the evening of life, our sight and hearing begin to fail, our bodies weaken, our power to move about may be restricted or taken from us. The body becomes rebellious, impatient, fatigued, and possessive. There are more frequent visits to medical facilities and health professionals. Bodily functions become a focus of new daily routines.

Will we fight this confining process or be humbled and learn from it? As an octogenarian recently told me, "In the twilight of life I choose the learning way, which is not one of guilt or regret, but more an awakening, an appreciation of the courage and receptivity that I have witnessed through the years by others who were aging.

"Strange: I managed somehow or another to avoid old age longer than most people. Perhaps this was possible because I carried some old age in me from early on. An automobile accident in childhood and subsequent disability, near death experience, being an only child of separated parents, raised mostly by a grand-mother—these tend to rob one of a natural easy youth and face one with some elements of old age very early on.

"Nevertheless, I arrived at age eighty-five with some extraordinary faculties and some very severe deficits. At the beginning of that year I was functioning mostly on my Puer energy, but by the end of the year I was limping about with severe symptoms of old age. This was painful, but it brought some new capacities that are pure joy.

"A dream during my eighty-fifth year outlines some of this transformation most clearly.

"*I dreamed that I awoke in another world that was entirely new to me. It was like a sudden arrival in the next world, a term frequently applied in my Baptist grandmother's religious mono-logues, carrying attached to it images of golden chariots, winged angels, streets of gold, divine choirs, and cherubs playing honeyed harps. I carried this vision of heaven too far into adulthood and paid a severe price for its promised happiness. The facts of my adulthood were very different from this golden motif and plunged me into different images. The dream visitation at age eighty-five placed me in a modest and even primitive house made entirely of brown adobe. It was earthen, with not a single straight line in its construction. There were a few people with me, all dressed in brown robes, standing about and not knowing who they were or what to do. I arrived in this new world initially in a similar state of confusion but shocked enough to know that I must pull out of this cloud of unknowing. I brought all the tools I knew to bear on this oblivion and quite suddenly awoke to who I was and the need to take responsibility for my situation. I went from one person to another, each as caught in oblivion as I had been, and I managed to arouse each person into his present identity.*

"This brought about a great happiness and capacity to see the beauty and great dignity that we were in. I then left this group and wandered about through many rooms, discovering unexpected beauty and contentment. It was all characterized by the earth-brown color of the material of the building and our clothing. It was not entirely without gold. There was brilliant golden sunshine everywhere, inside and out, but no specific source of light. Every-thing seemed to give forth its own radiance and power. The dream had no end, and it left me exploring this brown/golden radiant world.

"I was professionally trained to see dreams as most often offering some new information or correcting some misinformation one unknowingly carries within oneself. From this point of view, I think this dream was preparing me for another level of consciousness, cured of my grandmother's sentimentality and prejudice about heaven. The insistence on brown color (simplicity and naturalness), the absence of overwrought decoration, and the lack of any straight lines (straight being the symbol of a patriarchal, law-dominated culture) were the elements I needed to cure one-sidedness in the vision of paradise."

Finding True Paradise

The myth of paradise or a golden age has been prevalent in some form in every culture. All creation myths also recount the loss of paradise, the fall from unified consciousness into that splitting of reality that we contemporary people call neurosis. No paradise works in its literal sense, but this shouldn't discredit the idea of paradise. There are two types of paradise: One is the Garden of Eden, that wholeness that Castor and Pollux left when they gained consciousness. No one can go back to that golden age. Attempting to do so is a regression that does harm to our personality (and to our society).

The pull of the old paradise is particularly strong for adolescents (people can operate from adolescent consciousness at any age). In adolescence we are beckoned to step up to a new level of consciousness, but at the same time something in us yearns to go back, back to the "good old days," a lost paradise of innocence, simplicity, and mastery. This nostalgia sings its Lorelei song to us at various times throughout life. If you succumb to this pull, returning to an infantile paradise without incorporating anything from the realities of your experience and culture, then you have regressed. There are many physical as well as emotional illnesses that grow out of this regression.

To understand paradise, think about the different levels of consciousness: You have every right to ask for a paradise if you put it on the proper level. A second, or alternative, conception of paradise is what William Blake called "the Heavenly Jerusalem." We start in the Garden of Eden as a child and gradually lose this wholeness as we go through the differentiation process. While you can't go backward (consciousness continues to flow and move), you can go forward. In language we struggle to explain something that is truly beyond the inherent duality of language and the ego. So we must utilize a symbol that consciousness can make sense of, such as the progression from the innocent wholeness of Eden to the informed wholeness of the Heavenly Jerusalem.

In the final analysis there is only one paradise, and it was never lost or gained. You have heaven in your hands all the time. It is not some other time, another place, a different condition. You have the whole of paradise with you now, total, complete, and paid for. You must only clarify your vision to see it.

Paradise consists of reality looked at from a different consciousness. This seems a let-down at first. It does not come when you have earned it, but when you can stand it. A vision of paradise, when it comes too soon, is terribly painful. If you are touched by a bit of heaven and don't relate to it, that is, you don't make a reciprocal relationship with your divine potential, it can turn into an experience of hell.

One of the defining characteristics of paradise is that it occurs outside of time. Eternity doesn't begin when time stops. The origin of the Sabbath came from the recognized need to pull out of ordinary consciousness for one day each week. To make conscious our view of time is a key step toward enlightenment. Ask yourself: By what time reference do I live my life? Often our sense of happiness is diametrically opposed to our sense of the urgency of time.

The French post-impressionist painter Paul Gauguin, frustrated by lack of recognition at home and financially destitute, sailed to the tropics to escape European civilization and "everything that is artificial and conventional." (Before this he had made several attempts to find a tropical paradise where he could live on fish and fruit and paint in his increasingly primitive style, including short stays in Martinique and as a worker on the Panama Canal.) In 1891, Gauguin went to Tahiti, a projection of the literal paradise, thinking that would be the antidote to his alienated life in nineteenth-century Europe. When he arrived in the South Seas, he found that the physical reality was not what he expected; it included poverty, hunger, and disease. But through his quest he found a symbolic or interior paradise, which is what he painted and how we remember him.

Life is unendurable without an occasional taste of paradise. The infantile paradise in which Castor and Pollux are as one is built into us, but we all must leave that Garden of Eden; if you get too attached to that early state it is the end of your development. Later in life we fantasize about paradise, and that in itself is the worst possible barrier to realizing it.

It may seem like a terrible letdown to fully admit the truth. This truth is so essential that I must repeat myself: Paradise exists, but as a level of consciousness, and it is available to you when you are ready to receive it.

Spiritual teachings are sometimes interpreted as advising us to let go of material things and lighten our load by reducing attachments, but this is a fundamental misunderstanding of a profound truth. To advance consciousness we need to be weaned, not from material things, but from our allegiance to duality. The very idea that the material world is separate from some other "higher" existence is itself an error of duality. Reality is not dual, though our current level of awareness perceives it that way.

If a person comes to a point of integration or pulling together of the two realms, he or she doesn't obey the polarity of opposites as other people do. An enlightened person is not so limited and one-sided and is less of a specialist. This process of transitioning from our usual ego state to paradise consciousness, however, is fraught with danger. What often happens is that the ego just fakes surrender and then tries to assimilate the higher Self, and you end up with a king-sized inflation. It's been said that ninety-five percent of the teaching required for enlightenment is getting a structure that can stand it, and realization of paradise here on earth is almost an afterthought. It is most clear what you must guard against—don't inflate. To the ancients, the desire to know all—to be as a god—was a fatal desire.

You can see this in many of the so-called holy men and gurus who get a taste of paradise and then use it to gain power, accumulating followers and wealth and then abusing them. When it comes to real transformation, there is no possibility of assimilating paradise consciousness; it assimilates you.

People who come to this point in their development put up the most extraordinary excuses not to claim their piece of heaven. The whole essence of choice, characteristic of our egoic world, has preferences. We define ourselves through our struggles with these endless oppositions.

We talk about how to get "there," when, in fact, there is nowhere else to go. Buddhism states that reality is singular, never dual. Ordinary mind and Buddha mind are one. Christians attest to this, sometimes sleepily, every Sunday when reciting, "I believe in one God, the Father almighty, maker of Heaven and Earth . . ." This implies One God, not duality. In other words, all the apparent contradictions of life can be resolved, but this requires displacing the ego as the center of your universe.

The Judas Codex

Jesus is said to have told Judas, "You will exceed all of them. For you will sacrifice the man that clothes me."

I have criticized established religious institutions for failing to address the spiritual needs of modern humankind and failing to see the deeper aspects of their teachings. All conceptions of the divine are of necessity metaphors and symbols for that mystery and totality beyond knowing. It was Jung who woke me to the validity of the Church's claim that Christianity was a powerful portrayal of the psyche of Western humankind and a still relevant guide to the inner path. Jung, by his own admission, never entirely recovered from the wounds of his pastor father, but, still, it was Jung's work that gave me the key to understanding Christian teachings in a new way.

For Jung there was a basic contradiction within the Christian orthodoxy in the total exclusion of the dark side of the human condition. The recently rediscovered Judas Codex, that long-buried second-century writing that must have been on the long list of gospels that were considered for inclusion in an official canon of the Church, offers a point of view that could help us out of contradiction.

The observation that the Church has the huge task of ministering to a wide range of consciousness in its congregations softened my criticism of its teachings. I observed three main levels of consciousness that history has brought to the ministrations of the Church, each so widely different from the others that it is mind-boggling to gather them all up under one teaching.

The first level of consciousness is for a very primitive, mostly illiterate people who are best taught by law and authority. The second is our own condition, people who have minds of their own and demand freedom and democracy as their God-given right. The third level is the only now-appearing understanding that ego consciousness is not adequate for running the affairs of custom and government.

Is it any wonder that the Church shudders under the contradictions of these divergent needs?

The first two levels of consciousness desperately need law and order for safety. It was relatively easy to provide these until the

present time. A set canon, avoidance of contradiction, unequivo-
cal guideposts were essential. The Christian Church (and this
applies equally to other major religious institutions) set up a
system of rights and wrongs that were beyond human question.
This was best accomplished by having a rigidly defined hero and
antihero mythology: God and the Devil, Jesus and Judas, and on
down the scale to the cowboy hero and the villain, Luke Skywalker
and the Evil Emperor, and the latest duality of good and evil in the
celluloid myths of today.

Such a myth needed a betrayer and found him in Judas;
this descending scale of hero/antihero makes its way to this day
in America/Communism (now America/Fundamentalist Islam),
Catholic/Protestant, Jew/Gentile, Republican/Democrat, yuppie/
hippie, my family/the inconsiderate neighbors.

At its best, this collision of opposites gives science its power of
discrimination. At its worst, it keeps us in a constant warfare—
from international politics to our own private neurotic behavior. It
is clear that humankind cannot survive much longer in this eternal conflict, but the solution requires so radical an alteration in
basic attitude that it is questionable whether we will actually
achieve such a vast change in time to avert an apocalyptic (a word
originally meaning the up-rush of a new value more than the
collapse of an old one) crash.

One possibility on a mythological/religious level would be to
reinstate Judas from villain to hero. This is exactly what the Judas
Codex prescribes! The parchment records a conversation between

Jesus and Judas in which Jesus tells Judas to arrange for the crucifixion so that the Divine Redemption can take place. Jesus goes on to say that Judas will be the best or greatest of the twelve for doing this.

Oh my, what is this saying?

The divine path was to bring the disaster of the crucifixion to the level of redemption? The villain to the level of hero? Bad to the salvation of the failed good? The historical facts of this gospel will be debated by theologians, but we must focus on the psychological import of it coming forward at this particular point in history.

Jung prescribes this in no uncertain terms when he discusses the transformation of neurotic warfare into divine paradox. Using different terminology can help, but the fact is death knell to most of our treasured ideas of good and evil. Another way of saying this is to make use of an event long past in our history—the time when Copernicus got into trouble with the authorities for saying that the sun, not the earth, was the center of our universe. Copernicus won out on the historical level, but we proud, haughty moderns have not begun to make that same revolution concerning the centrality of ego (the organizing principle of consciousness) over the higher Self (an organizing principle that includes those aspects of us that are both lived and unlived, conscious and unconscious).

Jung wrote, "Modern man protects himself against seeing his own split state by a system of compartments. Certain areas of outer life and of his own behavior are kept, as it were, in separate drawers and are never confronted with one another . . . the sad truth is that man's real life consists of a complex of inexorable opposites—day and night, birth and death, happiness and misery, good and evil . . . Life is a battleground, and if it were not so, existence would come to an end."

And in a passage written near the end of his life: "Just as all energy proceeds from opposition, so the psyche too possesses its inner polarity, this being the indispensable prerequisite for its aliveness . . . Both theoretically and practically, polarity is inherent in all living things. Set against this overpowering force is the fragile unity of the ego. That an ego was possible at all appears to spring from the fact that all opposites seek to achieve a state of balance."[40]

Our language, which dominates so much of thought, can conceive of nothing but the play of opposites. At best, this produces delight, dance, drama—and paradox; but at worst, it produces doubt, anxiety, guilt, and contradiction. Modern humankind seems to have drifted more and more into the Hamlet state of suffering over choosing "To be, or not to be."

Does it then follow that we are destined to live the pain of being torn by dual choices so long as we choose to remain on the human level? Wolfgang Pauli (a noted scientist who was arguably second only to Einstein in the development of modern physics) once said, "My conscious cannot endure without a pair of opposites. Therefore, for me, the unity beyond consciousness will always be with the divine."

Coming Back Home

Many years ago while living in India I was confronted by an old yogi who said, "You will incarnate in every possible life form before you are finished." This seemed to imply that I would be a rich man, a poor man, a saint, a sinner. There would be incarnations to teach me everything that is humanly possible. This was followed by a long pause as he waited for the enormity of that statement to sink into my brain. Then he pointed at me and said, "You are in all of your incarnations simultaneously." Again there was a pause. Next he said, "That which is in all of its incarnations simultaneously is God." After a pregnant pause he looked me directly in the eye and delivered a line that sent me reeling: "And that is you!" Then he walked off. I have never been the same since.

The idea of reincarnation is a fanciful way of addressing unlived life. If we take it literally, it seems to suggest that we are reborn through time as different people or even animals. This is the ego's attachment to an identity. Literalism is always a form of idolatry, and the idol is usually our own ego. The ego can't imagine its transformation and so literalizes it. A living mystery is concretized into a concept, a belief rather than a lived experience. Understood psychologically, reincarnation refers to the redemption of our unlived life, the necessity of addressing all our potentials before we can realize God (unity). There are thousands of potentialities within, all of which are calling simultaneously to be expressed and experienced. This is the meaning of reincarnation for the modern person. All of our potentials want to be incarnated, to be lived out before our journey back to wholeness is complete. All of them are vying for attention simultaneously. Reincarnation is not for another time, another place, another existence—it is *now*. Understood at the proper level, we are in all our incarnations simultaneously. We embody divine consciousness.

Yet this realization of paradise is nearly always perceived by the ego to be a complete disaster. The ways of attempting to wriggle out of a potential enlightenment are legion. The mystical world is just too inconceivable for most people. But if you know what you are doing—it is sublime.

A key concern: What do you do after achieving enlightenment?

Surprisingly, the sages indicate that you do exactly the same thing you were doing before, but now you know what you are doing. Your doing is in service to being. The higher Self stands in the background and illuminates everything you do like a flash bulb. Anything looked at through your ego will continue to be an irresolvable pair of opposites, and this can only grind you down. But the same situation viewed through enlightened eyes can be seen as part of the creative play of God.

As Buddhism reminds us: Before enlightenment, chop wood and carry water. After enlightenment, chop wood and carry water.

Silently, a Flower Blooms

A Zen master from the East, Zenkei Shibayama, illustrates awakened awareness in verse:

Silently, a flower blooms,
In silence it falls away;
Yet here now, at this moment, at this place
The world of the flower, the whole of
the world is blooming.
This is the talk of the flower,
The glory of eternal life is
Fully shining here.[41]

We live in an era of growing anxiety, a dark night that precedes the light of the new dawn. As the wise old teacher in India once tried to instruct, all of the possible incarnations are within us—this is the call of unlived life, but will we respond? Only if we can learn to moderate our reflexive patterns, cease defending partial, provisional identities, and open to what is waiting beyond the known.

We live in a time of division and polarity, yet the ancients sagely advised that the middle way is best. This does not mean a watered-down compromise but a synthesis. Life is filled with contradiction and tension, and yet if we can learn to hold that tension rather than force one-sided solutions, we might yet open to experiences that are whole and holy. It need not be a cataclysm that shifts our awareness to a deeper level—if we look within.

In the socially driven process of becoming legitimate and gaining credentials for success in the world, in the experience of wielding power, through our hunger for certainties in a universe filled with paradox and mystery, we don't want to face our shadows and question our assumptions. It is easier to split off the "bad" onto our neighbors, whether they are down the street or across the ocean, to fear the "other" rather than face the "otherness" within.

Ask yourself the following questions: What is necessary for me to undertake the next stage of my journey? Can I give myself permission to explore new paths? How does fear keep me in a reactive stance, bound to outmoded ways of being? Am I content to live in a backwater of my personality, or am I ready to grow into new ways of thinking and feeling? Can I marshal the energy needed to realize my unlived potentials? Living the unlived life begins today, with you.

I have been touched by the words of Gilbert Murray, a scholar and translator of the Greek classics, who wrote, "Live in the service of something higher and more enduring, so that when the tragic transience of life at last breaks in upon you, you can feel that the thing for which you have lived does not die."

Notes

1. T. S. Eliot, "Little Gidding," in *Four Quartets*, copyright 1942 by T. S. Eliot and renewed 1970 by Esme Valerie Eliot, reprinted by permission of Harcourt, Inc.

2. C. G. Jung, *The Collected Works of C. G. Jung*, trans. R. F. C. Hull (Princeton, NJ: Princeton University Press, 1973), vol. 9, part 2, paras. 43–67. (*The Collected Works* are hereafter abbreviated CW.)

   The higher Self pushes us toward essential life experiences and connection to deeper and greater realms. Identity that is aligned with essential archetypal patterns of the cosmos produces what the ego experiences as meaning. The higher Self is more correctly used as a verb, as in "selfing," since it is neither static nor really a thing. It is an observable process, and in this book when we refer to the higher Self it should be understood as the propensity of psyche to dynamically seek greater levels of integration, organization, relationship, and creative expression.

   Self-organizing qualities of the psyche have been discussed extensively, particularly in complex systems theory. For those readers who are scientifically minded, it is worth noting that homeostasis, one of the fundamental characteristics of living things, is a property of open systems, especially living organisms, to regulate their internal environment to maintain a stable, constant condition by means of multiple dynamic equilibrium adjustments. The term was coined in 1932 by Walter Cannon from the Greek *homoios* ("same," "like," "resembling") and *stasis* ("to stand," "posture"). Your body, when working well, has built-in capacities to balance temperature, salinity, acidity, and the concentrations of nutrients and wastes within tolerable limits. This is self-regulation.

Similarly, the psyche has self-correcting and compensatory qualities. Since psychic processes are dynamic and do not regulate around fixed points (like a thermostat), a better term for describing them is homeorhesis. *Homeorhesis*, derived from the Greek for "similar flow," is a concept encompassing dynamic systems that return to a trajectory, as opposed to systems that return to a particular state (homeostasis). First coined by C. H. Waddington in 1940, homeorhesis is the quality of psyche to regulate itself around dynamic processes. In ecology this concept is utilized in the Gaia theory, where the system under consideration is the ecological balance of different forms of life on the planet. See C. H. Waddington, *Tools for Thought: How to Understand and Apply the Latest Scientific Techniques of Problem Solving* (New York: Basic Books, 1977). "Selfing," or the propensity of the higher Self to promote unlived potentials for integration and expression, can be understood through a scientific metaphor as well as religious metaphor, i.e., the divine spark or soul moving us closer to wholeness and divine manifestation.

3. Thomas Mann, "Freud and the Future," in *Essays* (New York: Vintage Books, 1957), p. 317.

4. The Unlived Life Inventory is modeled on a questionnaire originally developed by Roland Evans, and has been adapted for our uses with his assistance. For other useful therapeutic tools, see Evans's wonderful book *Seeking Wholeness: Insight into the Mystery of Experience* (Boulder, CO: Sunshine Press, 2001).

5. As quoted in Kate Hovey, "Castor and Pollux," www.The-Pantheon.com. My retelling of the myth of Castor and Pollux also draws upon numerous sources, most particularly:

Karl Kerenyi, *Gods of the Greeks* (New York: Thames and Hudson, 1980).

Jane Ellen Harrison, *Epilegomena to the Study of Greek Religion, and Themis: A Study of the Social Origins of Greek Religion* (New York: Meridian Books, 1955).

Gilbert Murray, *Five Stages of Greek Religion* (Mineda, NY: Dover Publications, 2003).

The Columbia Electronic Encyclopedia, 6th ed. (New York: Columbia University Press, 2006).

Arthur Cotterell, *The Encyclopedia of Mythology*. (New York: Anness Publishing, Ltd., 1996), p. 38.

Mike Dixon-Kennedy, *Encyclopedia of Greco-Roman Mythology*, (Santa Barbara, CA: ABC-CLIO, Inc., 1998), p. 116.

Pierre Grimal, ed., *Larousse World Mythology* (New York, G. P. Putnam's Sons, 1965), pp. 118–119.

Thomas Bulfinch, *Bulfinch's Mythology* (New York: Random House, 1993), p. 148.

6. C. G. Jung, CW, vol. 8, para. 749–795.

7. C. G. Jung, CW, vol. 7, para. 112. Jung, following Heraclitus, writes, "The only person who escapes the grim law of enantiodromia is the man (sic) who knows how to separate himself from the unconscious, not by repressing it—for then it simply attacks him from the rear—but by putting it clearly before him *as that which he is not.*"

8. C. G. Jung, CW, vol. 7, para. 114.

9. Antonio Machado, "Last night, as I was sleeping," from *Times Alone: Selected Poems of Antonio Machado*, trans. Robert Bly (Middletown, CT: Wesleyan University Press, 1983). Reprinted by permission of Wesleyan University Press.

10. James Hollis, *The Middle Passage: From Misery to Meaning in Midlife* (Toronto: Inner City Books, 1993). This, like all of Hollis's books, is rich and thought-provoking.

11. There is a similarity between the "strange attractors" of chaos theory and Jung's notion of psychological complexes. You may operate on the edge of certain states, and then comes a "tipping point." Attractors exhibit their self-iterating capacity in the psyche by demonstrating their attractive or seductive power as phenomena, ideas, theories, moods, and behaviors. These psychic nexus points are instrumental in the foundation of belief systems, emotional response, and behavior. A relevant article by J. May and M. Groder is "Jungian Thought and Dynamical Systems: A New Science of Archetypal Psychology,"

in *Psychological Perspectives,* Spring–Summer 1989, vol. 20, no. 1, pp. 142–155.

12. For a useful summary of recent research in the science of human emotions, see Thomas Lewis, Fari Amini, and Richard Lannon, *A General Theory of Love* (New York: Vintage Books, 2001).

13. From the egoic perspective so much of life seems to involve opposition and contradiction, while from the more encompassing view of greater consciousness the same world becomes filled with paradox, mystery, and awe. The optimal identities (in people and organizations) are capable of critiquing themselves and seeing through partial views of reality as just that—partial and limited. As Owen Barfield has observed, literalism is idolatry.

14. For a broader discussion of this point, please see Robert Johnson's book *Owning Your Own Shadow: Understanding the Dark Side of the Psyche* (San Francisco: HarperSanFrancisco, 1993).

15. To unravel the knot of one's complexes is a long-term and ongoing project. In analysis I often ask clients to purchase a journal notebook and three pens, each with a different color ink. Assign a color to each of the different ways we orient ourselves to the world: black ink to record your thoughts, red for feelings, blue for physical sensations. Take time at least once a week to write in your journal. This is a great way to let go of your day before sleeping, so if you need to justify the effort in your busy schedule, think of it as a sleep aid.

Check in with each of these different aspects of your experience.

Noticing your thoughts will be the easiest. Use your journal as a container to hold the ideas that frequently run through your mind. Then check in with your feelings and write them down in red ink. Next, focus your attention on your physical body: Start with your toes and slowly scan up to your ankles, calves, thighs, and so on until you get to your head. Notice any tight places where you hold tension. Observe where you are numb or where there is little awareness at all and write this down. Record what you observe in blue ink.

The colors of ink will reflect different aspects of your selfhood. If you keep up with this a journal for a month or more you will assemble a record of how you process experience. Just becoming conscious of how much ink of a particular color appears is highly instructive. Many people will have mostly black ink, indicating how much they live in their thoughts.

With this journal you will become familiar with the repetitive patterns of your complexes in action. Are there certain thoughts that come to you repeatedly? What is the relationship of thoughts to feelings? For example, do you become depressed when you tell yourself certain things? Are there old tapes that you play in your head upon waking each morning? What happens repeatedly when you are in a stressful situation? What messages infiltrate and shape your evaluations of reality and your decisions? Are you aware of your physical state when there is a conflict? Where do you hold tension in your body? What do you do with subtle intuitions: Do you notice them at all? Override them with your ego's agenda? Remember that bringing awareness to your inner patterns is enough to initiate change. As you read later chapters of this book you will learn how to dialogue with the complexes and thereby slow them down and alter their effects.

16. In the Zen Buddhist tradition it is customary for a master to ask a newcomer questions to probe his or her spiritual depth. A standard question, most commonly used for this purpose, is "Who are you?" This simple, seemingly innocent question is one that Zen disciples fear. It demands of us that we reveal immediately the reality of the "I" underlying the common usage of the first person pronoun—that is, the whole person. To consider such a question at depth demands of the disciple an immediate realization of the "I" as pure and unconditioned subjectivity. At the moment he turns his attention to his own self, the self becomes objectified. The pure self can be realized only through a total transformation of the ego into something different, functioning in a different dimension of human awareness. Please see Toshihiko Izutsu's insightful book, *Toward a Philosophy of Zen Buddhism* (Boulder, CO: Prajna Press, 1982).

17. Walt Whitman, *Song of Myself*.

18. Coleman Barks, "Rumi and the Celts: The Soul as Conversation and Friendship," *Parabola*, Winter 2004, p. 26.

19. What is more, though we all have a sense of what "I" means, on closer inspection it is very difficult to grasp, for the self is not a place or a thing. No "self" has ever been found on a CT-scan, in the dissection of a human

brain, or in our genetic code. The self is an ever-flowing, ever-changing process, so it would be more correct to refer to it as a verb rather than a noun. We are constantly in the process of "selfing," and though we possess a sense of continuity, at bottom there is no enduring "I" to be found.

20. Mary Watkins, *Invisible Guests: The Development of Imaginal Dialogues* (New York: Continuum International Publishing Group, 2000). This work contains an eloquent critique of developmental psychologies and their insistence on listening to only one voice per person. I have drawn upon her application of the term *imaginal*. Watkins is one of the original group who, with James Hillman, developed archetypal psychology in the 1970s.

21. Erving Goffman, *The Presentation of Self in Everyday Life* (New York: Anchor Books, 1959).

22. C. G. Jung, "The Aims of Psychotherapy," CW, vol. 16, paras 97, 98.

23. For more discussion of this point, see Robert Johnson's book *Inner Work: Using Dreams and Creative Imagination for Personal Growth and Integration* (San Francisco: HarperSanFrancisco, 1989).

24. C. G. Jung, "On the Secret of the Golden Flower." CW, vol. 13, para. 20.

25. Piero Ferrucci, *What We May Be* (New York: Tarcher/Penguin, 2004). This book provides a good introduction to psychosynthesis and exercises for development of one's imaginal capabilities.

26. C. G. Jung, CW, vol. 8, para. 532.

27. C. G. Jung, CW, vol. 16, para. 86.

28. Federico García Lorca, "Casida de la Rosa," trans. Jeremy Iversen. Reprinted with permission. Lorca was a Spanish poet and dramatist, also remembered as a painter, pianist, and composer. He was killed by Nationalist partisans at the beginning of the Spanish Civil War.

29. Russell Lockhart, "The Dream Wants a Dream," in *Psyche Speaks: A Jungian Approach to Self and World* (Wilmette, IL: Chiron Publications, 1987), p. 19.

30. Several of these techniques for phenomenological dream amplification are based upon the work of Stephen Aizenstadt, Ph.D., president of Pacifica Graduate Institute, Carpinteria, CA. Our thanks to Stephen for sharing his wisdom in seminars and conversations over the years. See Stephen Aizenstadt, *Dream Tending: Techniques for Uncovering the*

Hidden Intelligence of Your Dreams (audiotape, Sounds True Audio, 2002). For a practical application of the analytical insights of James Hillman for working with dream images, see Benjamin Sells, ed., *Working with Images: The Theoretical Base of Archetypal Psychology* (New York: Continuum International Publishing Group, 2000). See also James Hillman, *The Dream and the Underworld*. (New York: Harper & Row Publishers, 1979).

31. C. G. Jung, CW, vol. 7, p. 155, footnote.

32. There are now a number of dream incubation exercises posted on the Web. See also A. Bernard, "Dream Incubation" (Sherman Oaks, CA: California Family Conference, 1989).

33. For a wonderful exploration of play and its role in the arts and life, see Stephen Nachmanovitch, *Free Play* (New York: Tarcher, 1991).

34. C. G. Jung, CW, vol. 6, para. 197.

35. C. G. Jung, *Memories, Dreams, Reflections*, trans. Richard and Clara Winston (New York: Vintage Books, 1963), p. 174.

36. See Jung's introduction to Erich Neumann's *Depth Psychology and a New Ethic* (Shambhala, 1990).

37. For this insight and a useful discussion of contradictory versus contrary opposites I owe thanks to Jungian analyst Richard Sweeney and his unpublished paper "The Shadow Archetype and the Search for a New Ethic," presented March 17, 2007, and available from the Jung Association of Central Ohio, 59 W. 3rd Ave., Columbus, OH 43201.

38. William Blake, *Auguries of Innocence*

39. T. S. Eliot, "Burnt Norton," in *Four Quartets*, copyright 1940 by T. S. Eliot and renewed 1970 by Esme Valerie Eliot, reprinted by permission of Harcourt, Inc.

40. C. G. Jung, *Memories, Dreams, Reflections*.

41. Zenkei Shibayama, *A Flower Does Not Talk: Zen Essays* (Rutland, VT, and Tokyo, Japan: Tuttle Publishing, 1970). Reprinted by permission of Tuttle Publishing.

Appendix

Unlived Life Inventory

This exercise will help you to assemble an inventory of unlived life. You will see qualities that you have lived, possibilities that may have been cast off or closed to you, and potentials that you still would like to fulfill. Look for unrealized and underachieved potentials. While doing this exercise, direct your attention to the past in a reflective, honest manner, not idealizing it or judging it. It is what it is. Just state what has been true for you and what is true now.

Please read each statement carefully and take a few moments to decide on a true response for yourself. Then mark the box that most nearly reflects that response. Don't be concerned about scoring or the asterisks right now; just try to give each statement its own separate consideration.

The boxes offer a range of response from definitely disagree with the statement to definitely agree with the statement, as shown below:

DD - Definitely Disagree

SD - Somewhat Disagree

SA - Somewhat Agree

DA - Definitely agree

Outer Life

DD SD SA DA SCORE

1. I get satisfaction from what I do with my life.

2. I feel at ease relating to people.

3. New situations are difficult for me. *

4. My work life is not a good use of my talents

   and abilities. *

5. I have a positive attitude toward money.

6. I do not use my time effectively. *

7. My physical energy is good.

8. I feel overburdened with responsibility. *

9. I do not have enough free time for recreation

   and relaxation. *

10. I usually accomplish what I set out to do.

Outer Life Total:

Inner Life

	DD	SD	SA	DA	SCORE
1. I like myself as a person.	☐	☐	☐	☐	☐
2. I have (had) a loving relationship with my family of origin.	☐	☐	☐	☐	☐
3. I often experience difficult emotional states (sadness/anxiety/anger/stress).	☐	☐	☐	☐ *	☐
4. I feel uncomfortable when I am on my own.	☐	☐	☐	☐ *	☐
5. I keep a balance between looking after myself and looking after others.	☐	☐	☐	☐	☐
6. I find it difficult to concentrate and think clearly.	☐	☐	☐	☐ *	☐
7. I am able to show my love and affection to others easily.	☐	☐	☐	☐	☐
8. I feel dissatisfied with my personal relationship(s).	☐	☐	☐	☐ *	☐
9. I seldom know exactly what I am feeling.	☐	☐	☐	☐ *	☐
10. I have a positive relationship with my body.	☐	☐	☐	☐	☐

Inner Life Total: ☐

Deeper Life

	DD	SD	SA	DA	SCORE
1. I trust that I know what is best for me.	☐	☐	☐	☐	☐
2. I am able to express my creativity in a number of different ways.	☐	☐	☐	☐	☐
3. I am not interested in what goes on in my unconscious.	☐	☐	☐	☐ *	☐
4. I do not usually listen to my intuition and inner guidance.	☐	☐	☐	☐ *	☐

5. I cultivate a positive vision of my future.

6. I seldom pay attention to my dreams.

7. I know I am growing and developing.

8. I am not sure that I have the ability to heal myself.

9. I find it hard to imagine things I have never experienced.

10. I often feel connected to nature.

Deeper Life Total:

Greater Life

1. I am aware of the presence of a Higher Power (God/Life Force/Dharma/Tao).

2. I try to practice love and compassion toward others.

3. I am not sure that spirituality is important to me.

4. I do not believe that being alive has a greater purpose.

5. I want my life to have a positive impact on the world.

6. I do not have a regular spiritual practice (meditation/contemplation/prayer).

7. I spend time in activities that quiet my thoughts and feelings.

8. I easily get caught up in superficial activities and concerns.

DD SD SA DA SCORE

9. I seldom reflect on the meaning of my life
experiences. □□□□ * □

10. I follow what is spiritually "right" when making a
major decision. □□□□ □

Greater Life Total: □

Scoring

Questions 1, 2, 5, 7, and 10, in each section (without an *), are scored: 0, 1, 2, 3, from disagree to agree.

Questions 3, 4, 6, 8, and 9, in each section, marked with an *, are scored: 3, 2, 1, 0, from disagree to agree.

Sum the scores for each section and put the totals in the boxes below.

OUTER LIFE SCORE	
INNER LIFE SCORE	
DEEPER LIFE SCORE	
GREATER LIFE SCORE	
TOTAL SCORE	

Interpretation

Outer life is a dimension of external experiences and outer activity—how effectively and comfortably you approach the *doing* aspects of your life.

Inner life is a dimension of subjective experiences of your personal self—how you feel about yourself, your self-confidence, and your personal relationships with others.

Deeper life is the dimension of intuitive and creative experiences—how you relate to those aspects of your experience that seem outside conscious control.

Greater life is a dimension of the higher Self, transpersonal connection to the divine—how you relate to spirituality, core values, and aspirations.

Your score in each section is one measure of your realization and actualization of potential in that dimension.

Your total Whole Life Inventory score (out of a possible 120) gives a measure of the development and satisfaction you are experiencing in your life at present.

Scores of 15 or less in any section suggest that you have significant unlived and underdeveloped potentials in that area of your life. A measure of psychic health is your ability to experience different types of awareness and shift states (dimensions) with facility.

Your scores can help you to see where you may be over- or under-identified with certain aspects of your being. For example, you may be very comfortable with the outer dimension of life, the surface of the self, yet experience anxiety when you are required to move into inner experience (a realm that is key for feeling and relationships). Or you may score high in the greater dimension, but have difficulty paying the bills and keeping your outer life afloat. Highly spiritual people sometimes get lost in the transpersonal realm of experience.

The deeper dimension of life is the arena of symbolic impersonal knowing. Underlying consciousness, this is the foundation for your physical and psychological integration; if you scored low in the deeper dimension, review the questions again and consider how core beliefs developed from past experience may now be holding you back. Just for variety, listen to your intuition for your next decision or write down a dream to gain a different perspective.

You can use this framework—outer, inner, deeper, greater—to check in periodically with different aspects of yourself. What do you need right now to feel better? As you read through this book and develop more awareness, practice keeping an eye out for different dimensions of self-experience.

The goal is to keep a dynamic balance, accessing all the different possibilities of your self as you go through life. The path to wholeness is not about becoming cured or enlightened so much as managing different experiences and responding with resilience and creativity to life's ongoing changes. As you tune in to its different aspects, life becomes more interesting.

Comparing the scores for different dimensions gives a picture of the areas of your life that are more lived in contrast to areas that are relatively unlived. You can use the graph below to create a visual picture.

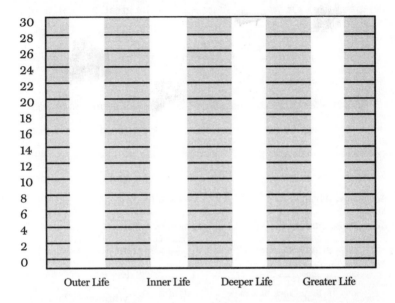

Reflect on which dimensions of your life would benefit from more attention, and notice areas in each dimension that seem to be least developed.

The Unlived Life Inventory provides you with a glimpse of your unlived life and will help to deepen your understanding and application of material discussed in the text. When you are finished reading the book, come back to the results of this inventory and consider what practical steps you can take during the next six months to develop new potentials and possibilities in your life.

Index

About the Authors

Robert A. Johnson is a world-renowned analyst, lecturer, and author of the bestsellers *He: Understanding Masculine Psychology* (HarperSan-Francisco, 1989, revised), *We: Understanding the Psychology of Romantic Love* (HarperSanFrancisco, 1985), and *Inner Work* (HarperSanFrancisco, 1989). His numerous books have been translated into nine different languages and can be found in libraries and bookstores on five continents. Johnson resides in San Diego, California.

Jerry M. Ruhl, Ph.D., is a clinical psychologist and a popular lecturer. In addition to his work in depth psychology, he has studied spiritual traditions in Japan, Bali, Thailand, Nepal, and India. His previous books include *Balancing Heaven and Earth* (HarperSanFrancisco, 1998) and *Contentment* (HarperSanFrancisco, 1999), both with Robert A. Johnson. Ruhl resides in Yellow Springs, Ohio, and maintains a private practice near Dayton, Ohio.

For more information on the authors and their seminars, books, tapes, and DVDs visit www.JerryRuhlRobertJohnson.com.